SOUTH DAKOTA
USA - 57106

The Preferred Jurisdiction
For Your Trust Needs

By
Monroe M. Diefendorf, Jr.
Argonne Trust Company, Inc.

Table of Contents

Introduction

Welcome to South Dakota and Argonne Trust Company.

This booklet is designed to highlight why South Dakota is the jurisdiction of preference when selecting the situs of a trust, along with why Argonne Trust Company should be your corporate trustee.

With technology and the expansion of the digital world, products and services that were once believed to be for the "rich and famous" are now available to and appropriate for "regular" people. Trusts fall into this category. And in March of 2012, Argonne Trust Company (ATC) was granted its trust charter from the Division of Banking from the State of South Dakota placing it into the mix for selection as corporate trustee.

Trusts come in all flavors and sizes and ATC is equipped to handle them all.

IRREVOCABLE TRUSTS

ILITS – Removes insurance proceeds from your estate and protects cash values during life and when you die from creditors

QPRTS – Transfer of residence while reserving right to live in home for a term of years and insulates the residence from your creditors claims

SST – Assets are protected from claims of beneficiary's creditors but when assets are distributed the lose protection

QTIP – Allows assets to pass to a spouse tax free but the ultimate distribution is not directed by spouse

CRT- Provides distribution of a percentage of trust principal and protects assets from a debtor spouse's creditors

CLT – Provides earnings above charity's payout to be distributed to grantor and assets are protected from creditors

GRAT – Grantor retains an annuity payment for a term of years and the annuity distributions to the non-debtor spouse are protected and cannot attach the GRAT principal

DAPT – settlor of the trust to be a discretionary beneficiary while protecting trust assets from the settlor's creditors.

But I will limit my overview by highlighting directed, dynasty and asset protection trust provisions.

This is designed to be a quick read, but with real content.

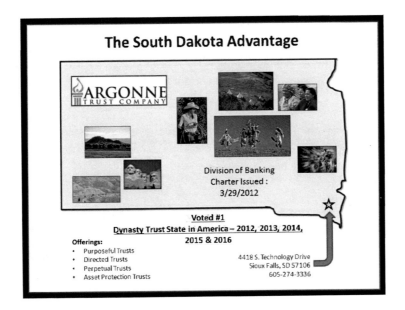

The South Dakota Advantage

Division of Banking
Charter Issued :
3/29/2012

Voted #1
Dynasty Trust State in America – 2012, 2013, 2014, 2015 & 2016

Offerings:
- Purposeful Trusts
- Directed Trusts
- Perpetual Trusts
- Asset Protection Trusts

4418 S. Technology Drive
Sioux Falls, SD 57106
605-274-3336

Directed Trusts

Directed trusts have existed for years, but they did not become statutorily recognized until 1986. And contrary to what some may believe, you don't have to live in one of these states to have a directed trust.

Generally speaking, a directed trust appoints;

    (1) a Trust Protector, who oversees the flow of the trust administration,

    (2) an Investment Committee, and

    (3) a Distribution Committee, made up of individuals (family) or a firm, who direct,

    (4) an Administrative Trustee, on either investment or distribution decisions. (See Appendix C for further details.)

With a directed trust, you can take advantage of the stability, longevity and experience of a well-established corporate trustee while placing the responsibility for certain decisions in another individuals (family) or firm.

Many individuals contemplating the establishment of a trust have a fear that by doing so they will be "locking in" or "tying up" their assets irrevocably. "Forever" decisions make it virtually impossible to draft a trust document that will make sense over time. I've heard it said that, "In perpetuity is a long time and things can change." To rectify this situation, a very powerful and important position, known as the "Trust Protector" was created.

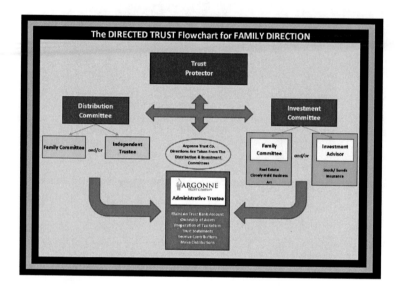

By way of background, South Dakota was the first state to enact a trust protector statute in 1997. A few additional states now allow for trust protectors. A "directed" trust in South Dakota often gives the following powers to a trust protector:

- Modify or amend the trust instrument to achieve favorable tax status or respond to changes in the Internal Revenue Code, state law, or the rulings and regulations there under.
- Increase or decrease the interest of any beneficiaries to the trust.
- Modify the terms of any power of appointment granted by the trust. However, a modification or amendment may not grant a beneficial interest to any individual or class of individuals not specifically provided for under the trust instrument.
- Remove and appoint a trustee, trust advisor, investment committee member or distribution committee member.
- Terminate the trust.
- Veto or direct trust distributions.

[6]

- <u>Change</u> situs or governing law of the trust or both.
- <u>Appoint</u> a successor trust protector.
- <u>Interpret</u> terms of the trust instrument at the request of the trustee.
- <u>Advise</u> the trustee on matters concerning a beneficiary.
- <u>Amend</u> or <u>modify</u> the trust instrument to take advantage of laws governing restraints on alienation, distribution of trust property or the administration of the trust.

Imagine? An "irrevocable" trust that can be changed by a protector! But relationships are often fickle. A trusted friend can sometimes turn into a foe over the smallest of issues. How can a grantor be assured that this position will not be abused? It's because the trust protector can be replaced at any time by the grantor. In fact, every position within the directed trust is part of a "checks and balances" system.

The Trust Protector can be commissioned or dethroned by the grantor. The Trust Company can be hired or fired by the Trust Protector. The Trust Company takes its direction from the Investment and Distribution Committees. The Investment and Distribution Committees can be modified by the Trust Protector. The Trust Company must follow the directions given by the grantor in the Trust Document. Each position has authority but each position is under the oversight of another position. It's like a Mexican standoff. Everyone must do their part as a fiduciary or they will be an ex-fiduciary. Brilliant.

But who should assume the position of Trust Protector? It can be a "trusted advisor," either an individual or LLC. So with this much "power," one's decision as to whom shall be the Trust Protector is important, but it's not irrevocable.

Who should NOT be a Trust Protector, as defined in § 1.672(c)-1 related or subordinate party of the SD code? This means the;
- grantor's spouse, if living with the grantor;
- the grantors father
- the grantors mother,
- the grantors issue,
- the grantors brother or sister;
- an employee of the grantor;
- a corporation or any employee of a corporation in which

the stock holdings of the grantor and the trust are significant from the viewpoint of voting control,

• or a subordinate employee of a corporation in which the grantor is an executive.

These persons are presumed to be subservient to the grantor in respect of the exercise or non-exercise of the powers conferred on them, unless shown not to be subservient by a preponderance of the evidence.

Perpetual Trusts

According to Investopedia, the definition of a dynasty trust is a long-term trust created to pass wealth from generation to generation without incurring transfer taxes such as estate and gift tax.

Trusts come in basically two flavors: limited term (lives in being plus 21 years) or dynasty (unlimited, in perpetuity).

The common law against perpetuities is not enforced in South Dakota. This means that a person can create a trust in South Dakota and avoid federal transfer tax system (gift and estate planning generation-skipping) forever, if a family chooses.

The following chart illustrates the value of avoiding estate transfer taxes after each generation. Without the tax confiscation on the trust assets, even a small $1 Million life insurance policy inside a SD ILIT can create truly a dynasty for your family.

Economics: Dynasty Trust vs. Outright Gift:		
[Assumptions - $1 million; trust lasts 120 years; 50% transfer tax every 30 years]		
After Tax Growth	Value of Dynasty Trust After 120 Years	Value of Property if No Trust
6.00%	$1,088,187,748	$68,011,734
7.00%	$3,357,788,383	$209,861,774
8.00%	$10,252,992,943	$640,812,059
9.00%	$30,987,015,749	$1,936,688,484
10.00%	$92,709,068,818	$5,794,316,801

So, if given the choice, which would you choose for your trust? No death taxes for a limited duration or no taxes forever? The answer is simple, but the execution of such a trust may not be as simple, as it may be beyond the experience of your local attorney. Remember, only

4 jurisdictions provide for trusts in perpetuity with NO income taxes (and New York is not one of them).

So, what is the best jurisdiction for your dynasty trusts? According to Trust and Estates Magazine, South Dakota has been rated "Best Trust Jurisdiction in the U.S." And, this esteemed publication has given South Dakota these additional ratings:

- Best Rule Against Perpetuity State

In addition, Steve Oshins has consistently ranked South Dakota as #1 in the Dynasty category since 2012 when the rankings began.

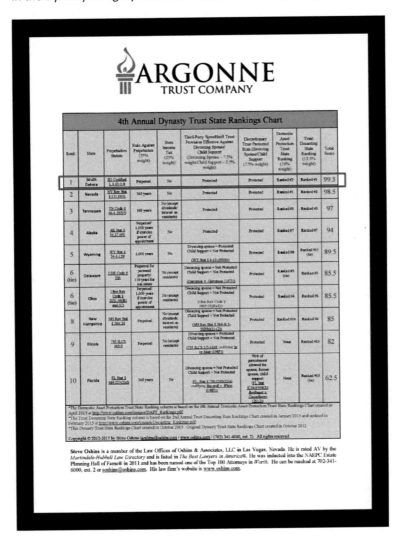

Asset Protection Trusts

In our litigious society, it is important to prepare for the inevitable event of being sued. The goal of asset protection is to reduce or eliminate losses to those who could claim them.

- Discourage lawsuits
- Provide an incentive for early and favorable settlements
- Level the playing field
- Add an element of control to the process
- Use of appropriate insurance products

In 2005, South Dakota enacted self-settled trust legislation statues to increase the states asset protection. South Dakota trusts are known to be free from complexities by statute. South Dakota offers some of the best asset protection in the United States.

South Dakota offers;

- Trust Statutes for protection
- Privacy protection
- Asset Protection for Life Insurance

There is controversy as to which provides the best asset protection, a regulated self-settled trust state or a non-regulated trust states. South Dakota is a regulated state and a regulated state is considered by many attorneys to be harder to pierce then a non-regulated state like Delaware and Nevada.

Steve Oshins consistently ranks South Dakota in the top two jurisdictions since the rankings began.

6th Annual Domestic Asset Protection Trust State Rankings Chart

Rank	State	State Income Tax (60% weight)	Statute of Limitations (Future Creditor) (5% weight)	Statute of Limitations (Preexisting Creditor) (5% weight)	Spouse/Child Support Exception Creditors (Spouse 3% weight/ Alimony 1% weight/ Child Support 1% weight)	Preexisting Torts Exception Creditors/Other Exception Creditors (5% weight)	Ease of Use - Is a new Affidavit of Solvency required for every new transfer? (7.5% weight)	Fraudulent Transfer Standard (5% weight)	Decanting State Ranking (7.5% weight)	Total Score
1	Nevada	No	2 Yrs.	2 Yrs. or 0.5 Yr. Discovery	No	No	No Affidavit Required	Clear and convincing	Ranked #2	99
2	South Dakota	No	2 Yrs.	2 Yrs. or 0.5 Yr. Discovery	Divorcing Spouse; Alimony; Child Support (only if existed at time of transfer)	No	No Affidavit Required	Clear and convincing	Ranked #1	98
3	Tennessee	No (except dividend/ interest on residents)	2 Yrs.	2 Yrs. or 0.5 Yr. Discovery	Divorcing Spouse; Alimony; Child Support	No	Affidavit Required	Clear and convincing	Ranked #3	86.5
4	Ohio	No (except residents)	1.5 Yrs.	1.5 Yrs. or 0.5 Yr. Discovery	Divorcing Spouse; Alimony; Child Support	No	Affidavit Required	Clear and convincing	Ranked #6	85
5 (tie)	Delaware	No (except residents)	4 Yrs.	4 Yrs. or 1 Yr. Discovery	Divorcing Spouse; Child Support	Preexisting Torts	No Affidavit Required	Clear and convincing	Ranked #5	79
5 (tie)	Missouri	No (except source income)	4 Yrs.	4 Yrs. or 1 Yr. Discovery	Alimony; Child Support	State RS In extent state/federal law provides	No Affidavit Required	Clear and convincing	Ranked #11 (tie)	79
7	Alaska	No	4 Yrs.	4 Yrs. or 1 Yr. Discovery	Divorcing Spouse	No	No Affidavit Required	Clear and convincing	Ranked #7	77
8	Wyoming	No	4 Yrs.	4 Yrs. or 1 Yr. Discovery	Child Support	Property listed on app. to obtain credit - but only as to that lender	Affidavit Required	Clear and convincing	Ranked #11 (tie)	75.5
9	Rhode Island	No	4 Yrs.	4 Yrs. or 1 Yr. Discovery	Divorcing Spouse; Alimony; Child Support	Preexisting Torts	No Affidavit Required	Clear and convincing	Ranked #10 (tie)	75
10	New Hampshire	No (except dividend/ interest on residents)	4 Yrs.	4 Yrs. or 1 Yr. Discovery	Divorcing Spouse; Alimony; Child Support	Preexisting Torts	No Affidavit Required	Limited clear and convincing evidence standard	Ranked #4	74.5
11	Hawaii	No (except residents)	2 Yrs.	2 Yrs. Pers. Injury; 6 Yrs. Contract	Divorcing Spouse; Alimony; Child Support	Preexisting Torts/ Certain Lenders/ Hawaii Tax	No Affidavit Required	Limited clear and convincing evidence standard	None	72
12	Utah	Very uncertain ability to avoid	None (immediate protection)	2 Yrs. or 1 Yr. Discovery (also 120 day mailing/ publication option)	No	No	Affidavit Required	Missing clear and convincing evidence standard	None	70*
13	Virginia	Yes	None (immediate protection)	5 Yrs.	Child Support	Creditors who have provided services to protect trust/ U.S Atty. etc.	No Affidavit Required	Clear and convincing	Ranked #8 (tie)	29.5
14	Oklahoma	Yes	4 Yrs.	4 Yrs. or 1 Yr. Discovery	Child Support	Must be majority Oklahoma assets	No Affidavit Required	Clear and convincing	None	16.5
15	Mississippi	Yes	2 Yrs.	2 Yrs. or 0.5 Yr. Discovery	Divorcing Spouse; Alimony; Child Support	Preexisting Torts; State/ Criminal Restitution/ Up to $1.5MM d/co $5MM Umbrella Policy	Affidavit Required	Clear and convincing	None	14.5

*6th Annual Domestic Asset Protection Trust State Rankings Chart created in April 2015. Original State Rankings Chart created in April 2010
Copyright © 2010-2015 by Steve Oshins (soshins@oshins.com / www.oshins.com, (702) 341-6000, ext. 2). All rights reserved.
*The Decanting State Ranking column is based on the 2nd Annual Trust Decanting State Rankings Chart created in January 2015 and updated in February 2015 at http://www.oshins.com/images/Decanting_Rankings.pdf.
*Utah's law is great for Utah residents, but is ranked low primarily because of its state income tax uncertainty for non-residents.

Steve Oshins is a member of the Law Offices of Oshins & Associates, LLC in Las Vegas, Nevada. He is rated AV by the Martindale-Hubbell Law Directory and is listed in The Best Lawyers in America® He was inducted into the NAEPC Estate Planning Hall of Fame® in 2011 and has been named one of the 24 "Elite Estate Planning Attorneys" by The Trust Advisor and one of the Top 100 Attorneys in Worth. He can be reached at 702-341-6000, ext. 2 or soshins@oshins.com. His law firm's website is www.oshins.com.

Total Seal

South Dakota is the only asset protection state that has a total seal on trust information forever. Clearly, this is also an important factor to consider when determining where to place an asset protection trust.

Bankruptcy vs. Creditor Protection

Bankruptcy - Occurs when your debts exceed all your assets, and you are insolvent.
Federal law applies (with some state law).

Creditor Protection - Occurs when someone has a judgment against you, but you aren't bankrupt
State law applies (with some federal law).

Business Entity Liability

Inside Liability - Problem originates inside your business *(when your truck driver gets drunk)*
Limited liability to personal and non-business assets.

Outside Liability - Problem originates outside your business *(when you get drunk)*
Unlimited liability to personal and business assets.

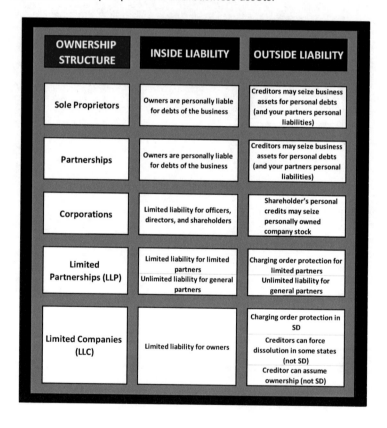

OWNERSHIP STRUCTURE	INSIDE LIABILITY	OUTSIDE LIABILITY
Sole Proprietors	Owners are personally liable for debts of the business	Creditors may seize business assets for personal debts (and your partners personal liabilities)
Partnerships	Owners are personally liable for debts of the business	Creditors may seize business assets for personal debts (and your partners personal liabilities)
Corporations	Limited liability for officers, directors, and shareholders	Shareholder's personal credits may seize personally owned company stock
Limited Partnerships (LLP)	Limited liability for limited partners / Unlimited liability for general partners	Charging order protection for limited partners / Unlimited liability for general partners
Limited Companies (LLC)	Limited liability for owners	Charging order protection in SD / Creditors can force dissolution in some states (not SD) / Creditor can assume ownership (not SD)

A Pre-Nup for your Heirs

Unfortunately, you know the statistics. Over fifty percent of all marriages end in divorce and the trend is moving upward. This makes divorce one of the greatest predators to wealth preservation. In fact, the average family of two children who each have two children will experience an average of 31 divorces over the next 100 years!

While we know this and we have been educated that the establishment of a pre-nuptial agreement will protect assets from the ravages of divorce, it is one conversation that we avoid like the plague. But even when we get the gumption to have "the difficult conversation" the results are not what we desire. It merely seems to throw fuel on the fire of division versus family unity.

I bet you have heard of an engagement terminated due to the introduction of a pre-nuptial. Or, perhaps you know a parent who suggested a pre-nup for a child and has been rebuked for this manipulation of the family wealth.

Pre-nuptials serve an important purpose but the side effects are sometimes more hurtful than helpful. So how do you accomplish the results you desire of protecting the family's wealth from divorce without the pre-nuptial?

As outlined above, South Dakota has the most favorable asset protection from creditors. But South Dakota has a "floating spouse" rule that provides trust benefits only while married. Upon divorce, the family assets are protected, similar to the asset protection of a creditor. Regardless of the number of times a family member is married, only the current spouse has benefits. In essence, a SD trust becomes a synthetic pre-nuptial.

Medicaid

In the event of loss of Medicaid, a self-settled trust may not be enough to create protection. To avoid loss of Medicaid when establishing a self-settled trust, it is not enough to create an irrevocable spend thrift trust, even if it is discretionary. South Dakota law like all other states are subject to 42 U.S.C. §1396p(d)(4), which explains how a trust can peacefully co-exist with Medicaid benefits. The beneficiary must be "disabled" as defined in the Social Security statute.

South Dakota is subject, like all states to the four dilemmas of self-settled trusts.

- The Full Faith and Credit Clause
- The Supremacy Clause of the US Constitution
- Fraudulent Conveyance
- Conflict of Law Arguments

South Dakota Asset Protection Statutes

55-1-25.

Distinction between discretionary trust and support trust--Creditor rights--Judicial review. (Source: SL 2008, ch 257, § 3).

The common law distinction between a discretionary trust and a support trust and the dual judicial review standards related to this distinction shall be maintained. In the area of creditor rights, the Restatement of Trusts (Third) and the Uniform Trust Code creates many new positions of law as well as adopts many minority positions of law. Sections 55-1-24 to 55-1-43, inclusive, affirmatively reject many of these positions. Therefore, the Legislature does not intend the courts to consult the Restatement (Third) of the Law of Trusts Articles § 50, § 56, § 58, § 59, or § 60 as approved by the American Law Institute of Uniform Trust Code Article 5 and Section 814(a) as approved by the National Conference of Commissioners on Uniform State Laws in 2004 with respect to subject matters addressed by §§ 55-1-24 to 55-1-43, inclusive.

55-1-26.

Judicial foreclosure of beneficial interests, powers of appointment, and reserved powers prohibited--Creditors may not reach powers of appointment or remainder interests. (Source: SL 2007, ch 280, § 2).

Regardless of whether or not a trust contains a spendthrift provision:
(1) No beneficial interest, power of appointment, or reserved power in a trust may be judicially foreclosed;
(2) No creditor may reach a power of appointment or a remainder interest at the trust level. The creditor shall wait until the funds are distributed before the creditor may reach the funds; and
(3) No power of appointment is a property interest.

55-1-27.

Certain remainder interests not property interests. (Source: SL 2007, ch 280, § 3; SL 2009, ch 252, § 3).

Although a remainder interest may be an enforceable right, where it is not absolutely certain based on the language of the trust that the remainder interest will be distributed within one year, it may not be classified as a property interest. This section does not affect eligibility for any public assistance program administered by the Department of Social Services pursuant to § 28-1-1.

55-1-28.

Removal or replacement power over trustee not exercisable by beneficiary's creditors--Interests of trustee beneficiary not reachable. (Source: SL 2007, ch 280, § 4).

No creditor may reach an interest of a beneficiary or any other person who holds an unconditional or conditional removal or replacement power over a trustee. This power is personal to the beneficiary and may not be exercised by the beneficiary's creditors. No court can direct a beneficiary to exercise the power.

No creditor may reach an interest of a beneficiary who is also a trustee or a co-trustee, or otherwise compel a distribution because the beneficiary is then serving as a trustee or co-trustee. No court may foreclose against such an interest.

55-1-29.

Trust property not subject to personal obligations of trustee. (Source: SL 2007, ch 280, § 5; SL 2009, ch 252, § 4).

Trust property is not subject to the personal obligations of the trustee, even if the trustee becomes insolvent or bankrupt.

55-1-30.

Distribution and remainder interests not relevant to division of marital property. (Source: SL 2007, ch 280, § 6).

Neither a distribution interest nor a remainder interest are relevant in the equitable division of marital property.

55-1-31.

Resources of settlor's spouse to be considered in making distribution from support trust--Other beneficiary's resources need not be considered. (Source: SL 2007, ch 280, § 7; SL 2008, ch 257, § 4).

Unless otherwise provided in the trust, if the settlor's spouse is named as beneficiary, while the settlor's spouse is still living, and the trust is classified as a support trust, then the trustee shall consider the beneficiary's resources, including the settlor's obligation of support, prior to making a distribution. In all other cases, unless otherwise provided in the trust, the trustee need not consider the beneficiary's resources in determining whether a distribution should be made.

55-1-32.

Factors which are not dominion and control over trust. (Source: SL 2007, ch 280, § 8; SL 2009, ch 252, § 5).

In the event that a party challenges a settlor or a beneficiary's influence over a trust, none of the following factors, alone or in combination, may be considered dominion and control over a trust:

(1) The settlor or a beneficiary serving as a trustee or a co-trustee as described in § 55-1-28;

(2) The settlor or a beneficiary holds an unrestricted power to remove or replace a trustee;

(3) The settlor or a beneficiary is a trust administrator, a general partner of a partnership, a manager of a limited liability company, an officer of a corporation, or any other managerial function of any other type of entity, and part or all of the trust property consists of an interest in the entity;

(4) A person related by blood or adoption to the settlor or a beneficiary is appointed as trustee;

(5) The settlor's or a beneficiary's agent, accountant, attorney, financial advisor, or friend is appointed as trustee;

(6) A business associate is appointed as a trustee;

(7) A beneficiary holds any power of appointment over any or all of the trust property;

(8) The settlor holds a power to substitute property of equivalent value;

(9) The trustee may loan trust property to the settlor for less than a full and adequate rate of interest or without adequate security;

(10) The distribution language provides any discretion; or

(11) The trust has only one beneficiary eligible for current distributions.

55-1-33.

Factors which are insufficient evidence that settlor controls or is alter ego of trustee. (Source: SL 2007, ch 280, § 9; SL 2009, ch 252, § 6).

Absent clear and convincing evidence, no settlor of an irrevocable trust may be deemed to be the alter ego of a trustee. The following factors by themselves or in combination are not sufficient evidence for a court to conclude that the settlor controls a trustee or is the alter ego of a trustee:

(1) Any combination of the factors listed in § 55-1-32;

(2) Isolated occurrences where the settlor has signed checks, made disbursements, or executed other documents related to the trust as a trustee, when in fact the settlor was not a trustee;

(3) Making any requests for distributions on behalf of beneficiaries;

(4) Making any requests to the trustee to hold, purchase, or sell any trust property.

55-1-34.

Provision that beneficial interest in trust income or principal may not be transferred before payment to beneficiary permissible. (Source: SL 2007, ch 280, § 10).

A settlor may provide in the terms of the trust that a beneficiary's beneficial interest in a trust's income, principal, or in both, may not be voluntarily or involuntarily transferred before payment or delivery of the beneficial interest to the beneficiary by the trustee.

55-1-35.

Declaration that beneficiary's interest subject to a spendthrift trust sufficient to restrain alienation by beneficiary. (Source: SL 2007, ch 280, § 11).

A declaration in a trust that the interest of a beneficiary shall be held subject to a spendthrift trust is sufficient to restrain voluntary or involuntary alienation of a beneficial interest by a beneficiary to the maximum extent provided by law.

55-1-36.

Conditions under which creditors of settlor beneficiary not prevented from satisfying claims from settlor's interest in trust.

(Source: SL 2007, ch 280, § 12).

If a settlor is also a beneficiary of the trust, a provision restraining the voluntary or involuntary transfer of the settlor's beneficial interest does not prevent the settlor's creditors from satisfying claims from the settlor's interest in the trust estate, unless the transfer specifically references and is qualified as a transfer under chapter 55-16. However, a settlor's creditors may not satisfy claims from either assets of the trust because of the existence of a discretionary power granted to the trustee by the terms of the trust instrument creating the trust, or any other provisions of law, to pay directly to the taxing authorities or to reimburse the settlor for any tax on trust income or principal which is payable by the settlor under the law imposing such tax; or reimbursements made to the settlor or direct tax payments made to a taxing authority for the settlor's benefit for any tax or trust income or principal which is payable by the trustor under the law imposing such tax.

Hybrid DAPT

For most professional individuals, there are few things more important than protecting their assets. These individuals work hard and long hours to accumulate wealth. With one claim, a majority of the individual's wealth can be taken by a creditor. Asset protection planning is about making it difficult or impossible for a creditor to get personal and business assets. Asset protection is not about fraudulently hiding or concealing assets from creditors. The focus for asset protection planning should be on protecting an individual's assets far in advance of a creditor claim and keeping the individual's assets after the creditor issue is resolved.

Although trusts have been routinely used as estate planning tools for generations, trusts have also become important asset protection vehicles. In most states, a person cannot create a trust, be a permissible beneficiary and have those trust assets be protected from creditors. South Dakota is one of the states that allow self-settled trusts otherwise known as Domestic Asset Protection Trusts ("DAPTs"). In very simple terms, a DAPT is an irrevocable trust an individual (commonly referred to as the Grantor) creates during his or her life and retains the right to be a discretionary beneficiary of the trust. If the DAPT is structured properly, the assets inside the trust are protected from the claims of the Grantor's creditors. The key with the DAPT is that, although the trustee has the discretion to make payments to or on behalf of the Grantor, the Grantor has no power to compel the trustee to make such payments. The legal theory is that if the Grantor cannot compel the trustee to make a distribution, no court can order the trustee to pay a Grantor's creditors.

Generally, to qualify as a DAPT under South Dakota's rules, the trust must be irrevocable, expressly incorporate South Dakota law, and have an independent trustee or co-trustee located in South Dakota. Additionally, part of the trust property should be located in South Dakota and all or part of the trust administration should be performed in South Dakota.

Why should a person considering a DAPT choose South Dakota? South Dakota offers a number of unique advantages. South Dakota has some of the best trust privacy laws; it does not have a Rule Against Perpetuities, which means a trust can technically go on forever here; it has some of the best decanting and trust reformation/modification laws, and finally, South Dakota does not have a state income tax, state corporate income tax, state capital gains tax, or state estate, gift or inheritance tax.

Although DAPTs have been used for a number of years, there has yet to be a single DAPT that has been tested all the way through the court system. Most estate planning attorneys believe that DAPTs, if structured properly, will provide asset protection for the Grantor. Because DAPTs have not been tested all the way through the court system, some commentators believe that DAPTs do not work for individuals who are not residents of the DAPT state. The argument is that a court in the home state of the individual (which doesn't recognize DAPTs) might decide that its law—not South Dakota law—applies and order the trustee to pay a creditor, even if the claim is not one that is recognized under South Dakota law. To help ensure asset protection, a new tool has been developed by Steven J. Oshins, a prominent estate planning attorney from Nevada. The new tool developed by Mr. Oshins is known as the Hybrid DAPT.

The Hybrid DAPT is similar to a regular DAPT, with one exception.

Initially, the Grantor is not a beneficiary of the trust, but can be added by an independent trustee or trust protector later. Typically, the trust is initially set up for the benefit of the Grantor's spouse and children. By not including the Grantor as a beneficiary of the trust, the Hybrid DAPT is a third-party trust (and not a self-settled trust) and therefore almost certainly avoids the potential risk of uncertainty of a regular DAPT.

Although not named directly in the trust as a beneficiary, the Grantor has indirect access to the trust assets through the spouse. The trust agreement can define the term "spouse" by using a "floating spouse provision" which defines the spouse as the person the Grantor is married to and living with from time to time. This gives the Grantor the ability to access the trust assets through a subsequent spouse in the event of a divorce or the death of the Grantor's current spouse.

If the Grantor doesn't have a spouse or child that will "share" a distribution with the Grantor and the Grantor needs a distribution, the trust agreement provides that the trust protector or independent trustee can add additional beneficiaries, including the Grantor. The trust protector or independent trustee will also have the right to subsequently remove the Grantor as a beneficiary well in advance of any potential creditor issue.

A DAPT (or Hybrid DAPT) can be structured in many different ways depending on the Grantor's income, estate, gift, and generation-skipping tax objectives. A DAPT can be structured so that transfers to the DAPT are considered completed gifts so that the future appreciation on the transferred assets is excluded from the Grantor's taxable estate. Alternatively, the DAPT may be structured so that no gift is made upon the transfer of property to the DAPT in order to preserve the Grantor's remaining estate or gift tax exemption. As a result, the contributed assets to the DAPT will remain in the Grantor's estate for estate tax purposes. Many DAPTs are structured so that the DAPT is considered a grantor trust for income tax purposes. If the DAPT is structured as a grantor trust for income tax purposes, the trust's income tax is paid by the Grantor.

By Christopher L. Fideler (chris@capflaw.com)

Foreign Nationals Trust Planning

		Grantor														
A		US Non-Domiciled								US Domiciled						
		Non-Citizen (NRA)				US Citizen				Non-Citizen (RA)				US Citizen		
		Spouse				Spouse				Spouse				Spouse		
B	Non-Citizen (NRA)	Non-Citizen (RA)	US Citizen - US Non-Domicile	US Citizen - US Domiciled	Non-Citizen (NRA)	Non-Citizen (RA)	US Citizen - US Non-Domicile	US Citizen - US Domiciled	Non-Citizen (NRA)	Non-Citizen (RA)	US Citizen - US Non-Domicile	US Citizen - US Domiciled	Non-Citizen (NRA)	Non-Citizen (RA)	US Citizen - US Non-Domicile	US Citizen - US Domiciled
INCOME TAX	n/a			Based on Residency*			Based on Residency*	Taxed on US Situs Assets Only			Based on Residency*					Based on Residency*
GIFT TAX	SD Exemption			Based on Domicile / Taxed on all World Wide Assets**			Based on Domicile / Taxed on all World Wide Assets**	$145,000 Exemption (not to trust) / QDOT			Taxed on all World Wide Assets / $145,000 Exemption					Taxed on all World Wide Assets / $5,340,000 Exemption
ESTATE TAX	US Situs Assets Only*** / $60,000 Exemption		US Situs Assets Only** / $60,000 Exemption	Taxed on all World Wide Assets / $60,000 Exemption			Taxed on all World Wide Assets / $5,340,000 Exemption	Taxed on all World Wide Assets / $5,450,000 Exemption / QDOT			Taxed on all World Wide Assets / $5,340,000 Exemption	Taxed on all World Wide Assets / $5,430,000 Exemption / QDOT				Taxed on all World Wide Assets / $5,340,000 Exemption

* Residency = (1/6 X # of days past 2 yrs) + (1/3 X # of days past 1 year) + (# of days current year) > $182 Days
** Gifts of intangibles are not subject to gift taxes - Gifts of RE & Cash are subject to gift taxes.
*** Cash & Life Insurance are not considered US Situs assets (U is not taxed in US for Non-US Citizens)

ARGONNE TRUST COMPANY

Foreign Law Trusts

Argonne Trust Company may be able to act as a directed and/or delegated trustee for trusts that are governed by foreign (non-U.S.) law, but administered in the U.S.
Some of the benefits include:

- A stable domestic corporate trustee
- Professional trust administration
- Possible reduction of exposure to sovereign risks
- Ability to reform the trust for administrative purposes pursuant to SD statute

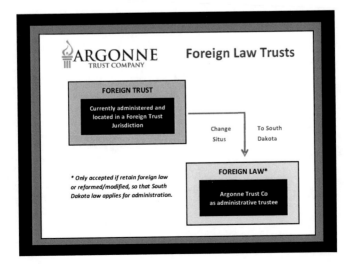

The South Dakota NRA Dynasty Trust

The South Dakota NRA (Non-Resident Alien) Dynasty Trust is a strategy for foreign citizens with U.S. citizen and/or green card children, grandchildren, and great grandchildren (whether born or unborn). The benefits of an NRA Dynasty Trust include the following:

- The NRA foreign citizen parent/grandparent can transfer an unlimited amount of assets on-shore into the trust without gift, death, or generation-skipping taxes.
- Assets are not subject to state income tax with Argonne Trust Company as trustee.
- The life insurance investment option (traditional or PPLI) is frequently chosen for the trust, thereby also avoiding federal income taxes within the trust. The life insurance option may also provide for federal and state income-tax-free withdrawals for the U.S. beneficiaries.
- South Dakota has the lowest state insurance premium tax (.08% for premiums over $100,000).
- The Dynasty Trust can continue <u>forever</u> for the benefit of U.S. beneficiaries and provide creditor protection.
- No Generation Skipping Tax or Gift Tax upon trust funding.

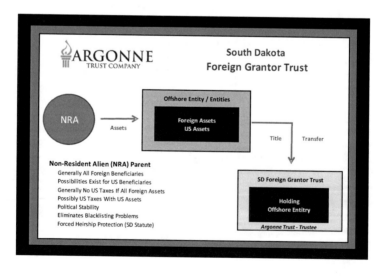

Stand-By South Dakota Dynasty Trusts

The Stand-by South Dakota Dynasty Trust is a strategy for foreign citizens with U.S. beneficiaries who have established foreign trusts in off-shore jurisdictions. Upon the grantor's death, the foreign trust pours the trust assets over to an existing (nominally funded) Stand-by South Dakota Dynasty Trust. This strategy could help to avoid the burdensome income tax filing requirements of the U.S. beneficiaries and the negative U.S. income tax rules on distributions of accumulated income.

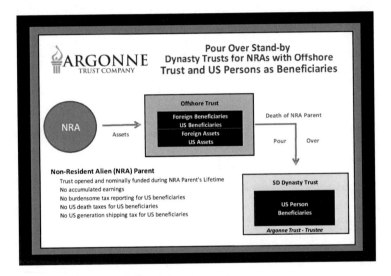

Pre-Immigration Planning

Substantial planning opportunities exist for Non-Resident Aliens (NRA) who anticipate immigrating to the U.S.:

- <u>Prior to immigration,</u> a NRA may generally make unlimited transfers to a South Dakota Self-Settled Trust with the NRA as a permissible beneficiary without incurring any U.S. transfer tax.

- <u>After immigration,</u> if the Grantor as a permissible beneficiary needs assets, they can generally be distributed by an Independent Trustee. If properly structured, the assets may be excluded from one's estate and protected from creditors and lawsuits.

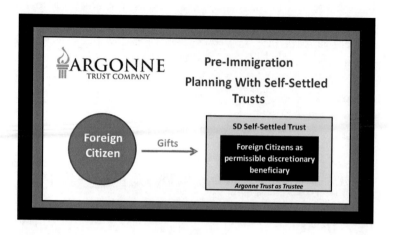

Qualified Domestic Trusts (QDOT)

Qualified Domestic Trusts were created under the Technical & Miscellaneous Revenue Act of 1988 (TAMRA), effective for decedents dying after November 10, 1988. Prior to TAMRA, the unlimited marital deduction was not allowed when property passed to a surviving spouse who was not a United States citizen. The <u>creation of **QDOT**s was designed to provide a mechanism whereby property could pass to a non-U.S. citizen spouse and still qualify for the unlimited marital deduction</u>. It is designed to achieve a very particular goal: deferring federal estate taxes when a U.S. citizen dies and leaves a large amount of money to a spouse who is not a U.S. citizen. If your family circumstances include both a lot of money—we're talking at least several million—and a non-citizen who might inherit it, you'll probably want to look into a QDOT.

The Estate Tax Problem for Non-citizens

Why do you need a special kind of trust if you're married to a non-citizen? When both members of a married couple are U.S. citizens, the first spouse to die can leave any amount of money to the survivor, completely free of estate tax. This is called the unlimited marital deduction.

The marital deduction does not apply, however, if the surviving spouse is not a citizen. A non-citizen survivor must pay estate tax just like anyone else who inherits. If the taxable estate is very large—more than $5.45 million, for deaths in 2016—then federal estate tax may be due. To avoid paying estate tax at the death of the first spouse, couples have two main options: get U.S citizenship for the non-citizen spouse or create a QDOT trust.

How a QDOT Works to Defer Estate Tax?

With a QDOT, at the first spouse's death, assets go to the trust instead of to the surviving non-citizen spouse. The survivor receives benefits (such as interest generated by trust bank accounts) from the trust assets, but doesn't own them. When the second spouse dies, assets pass to other beneficiaries named in the trust document—typically, the couple's children. If the estate is valuable enough, estate tax is paid then, as if the assets were in the estate of the first spouse to die. Trust assets are not included in the estate of the second spouse to die.

To get this tax break, detailed IRS rules must be followed when the trust is set up. For example, the trustee, who has control over the trust assets, must be a U.S. citizen. If the amount of trust assets exceeds $2 million, one of the trustees must be a U.S. bank. (If it isn't, the trustee must put up bonds for much of the trust's value.) And after the first spouse dies, the executor must choose, on the federal estate tax return filed for the deceased spouse's estate, to qualify for the marital deduction. This is called "making a QDOT election" and is irrevocable. The return must be filed nine months after the death.

The surviving spouse is entitled to receive any income earned by trust assets, and typically, all income is distributed to the survivor at least annually. These distributions are subject to income tax, but not estate tax.

If the trustee gives the surviving spouse any of the trust principal—the assets that were put in trust—estate tax may be due. However, if money is distributed in circumstances that fall under the IRS hardship exemption - no estate tax will be due. If the spouse has an "immediate and substantial" need for money relating to "heath, maintenance, education or support"—either his or her own, or that of someone he or she is legally obligated to support—a distribution of trust funds may qualify for a hardship exemption if the surviving spouse doesn't have other reasonably available liquid assets. (26 CFR § 20.2056A-5(c)(1).)

Purpose of the QDOT

The intent of the QDOT legislation is to preserve the marital deduction to ensure that a non-citizen spouse does not leave the United States with assets inherited without paying federal estate tax on those assets.

Requirements for a QDOT

To qualify as a QDOT, the trust must meet the following requirements:

- The executor must <u>elect on the estate tax return</u> to treat the trust as a QDOT.
- Every <u>distribution of principal</u> from the QDOT to the surviving spouse during her lifetime or at her death <u>will be subject to payment of estate tax</u>, and this tax is computed as if the distributions were included and taxed in the first spouse's estate.
- The terms of a QDOT should provide that <u>all income is distributable to the surviving non-citizen spouse</u>.
- The trustee of the QDOT must be a citizen of the United States.
- If the <u>QDOT assets exceed $2 million, then one of the trustees must be a U.S. bank *(like Argonne Trust Company)*,</u> and if there is an individual trustee, he or she must post a bond or letter of credit to the IRS in the amount of 65 percent of the value of the trust assets to secure payment of the tax.
- If the trust assets are under $2 million, then no bond need be posted and a U.S. bank need not be a trustee. However, <u>if more than 35 percent of the trust assets consist of real estate located outside the U.S a U.S bank trustee *(like Argonne Trust Company)*, is necessary</u>.

Planning Considerations

- To avoid the difficulties associated with QDOTs, it is advisable for clients to make use of the $148,000 gift tax exemption for 2016 available for transfers to a non-citizen spouse.
- Taxpayers may also consider purchasing sufficient life insurance within an irrevocable life insurance trust that can provide for the estate tax upon the death of the (citizen) spouse. The use of the life insurance to pay the estate tax would avoid having to use a QDOT.
- A QDOT need not be created in the decedent's will (or in a revocable living trust); it may be created by the surviving non-citizen spouse provided it is funded prior to the due date for the federal estate tax return.
- It is imperative to learn of the client's citizenship and status to accurately plan and determine if any estate tax treaties apply.
- If the surviving non-citizen spouse becomes a citizen prior to the filing of the estate tax return, there will be no need for a QDOT.
- If the surviving spouse becomes a citizen after the assets are transferred to the QDOT, distribution of property from the QDOT will not be taxed if:
    - The surviving spouse either was a U.S. resident from the date of death of the decedent or no taxable distributions were made from the QDOT prior to the surviving spouse becoming a citizen; and
    - The United States trustee notifies the IRS that the surviving spouse has become a U.S. citizen.
    - Special rules apply if the QDOT had already made taxable distributions.
- A QDOT Rollover IRA should be considered for the decedent's IRA and 401(k) assets to avoid an immediate income tax and estate tax.
- Joint property owned by the decedent and the non-citizen spouse will follow the rules established, which basically state that the asset will be includible in the gross estate of the person who paid for the asset.

- The QDOT should only be funded with assets in excess of the federal estate tax limit.

Tax Consequences

- The QDOT should be taxed as a simple trust for income tax purposes.
- The assets transferred into the QDOT are eligible for the unlimited marital deduction.
- Each distribution from the QDOT triggers the federal estate tax.
- Form 706-QDT must be filed annually to report the amount in the trust as well as the distributions made from the trust.
- A non-citizen spouse cannot use the applicable exclusion amount to shelter any distributions of principal from a QDOT, because QDOT assets are never considered part of the non-citizen spouse's gross estate; they are part of the deceased spouse's estate for estate tax purposes.
- A non-citizen spouse cannot use the applicable exclusion amount to shelter assets in a QDOT from estate taxes upon his or her death. However, the surviving non-citizen spouse may use the applicable exclusion amount ($5,450,000 in 2016) to shelter his or her own assets from federal estate taxes.

Using a South Dakota Trustee

The Division of Banking of South Dakota has granted Argonne Trust Company, Inc., a charter which allows for us to be your QDOT trustee. Along with our administrative expertise, all of the advantages afforded to clients through the South Dakota trust laws make Argonne Trust an excellent trustee solution when a QDOT is desirable.

Moving Your Foreign Residence to South Dakota

Do you own a home in a country outside the US? Perhaps it's a family residence that has been passed down through the generations. What a great asset to have – or is it? Let me suggest that it may be a liability rather than an asset without proper titling.

Did you know that assets owned outside the US must be included in your taxable estate when you die? I have heard some say "I have instructed my family not to say anything. Who will know?" It may be true that no one (not even the IRS) will know, however, failing to report your total taxable assets to the Internal Revenue Service may result in garnished wages to collect back taxes along with penalties, interest, fines and even imprisonment. So ignoring the regulations requires one to falsify information to the government. Is this the legacy that you wish to perpetuate to your heirs – lie on your tax returns?

But the procedure for identifying foreign assets has been formally passed. In March of 2010, the **Foreign Account Tax Compliance Act (FATCA)** was signed into law to reduce tax evasion by U.S. individuals with respect to income from financial assets held outside the United States. It requires foreign financial institutions to report information to the U.S. Internal Revenue Service (IRS) on such assets held directly or indirectly by U.S. taxpayers. Individuals also may be impacted by some lesser-known provisions of the new law. Individuals filing U.S. income tax returns will face new requirements to report foreign financial accounts and assets on a schedule attached to their Form 1040 (See Appendix D). Investments by U.S. individuals in foreign investment funds will be subject to additional reporting. U.S. individuals who create foreign trusts also will be subject to increased reporting and other rules affecting these trusts. Beginning 1/1/2013, the first phase of **FATCA** goes into effect. The next phase in 2014 will be the implementation of the withholding requirement and in January 2015, we will see additional withholding with respect to gross proceeds of sales. Bottom line – your foreign residence will be on the IRS radar screen.

One other "issue" may arise should there be multiple owners of the foreign residence. How will the ownership of the residence be transferred to successor generations? What happens when you have multiple families as owners? If you have a have a foreign residence I know you have thought about this (or even agonized over this).

Is there a better way to structure your foreign residence? Absolutely. Why do I know this? Because I am G-11 (the 11th generation of a family home located in Northern Italy and built in 1580). Here's how we have rectified "the problem."

    1) We created a South Dakota LLC.

    2) We got a valuation for the home and property.

    3) The individual owners of the home gifted the title of the asset into the LLC.

    4) We created a South Dakota Dynasty Trust (a trust that can hold real estate in perpetuity).

    5) The South Dakota LLC was gifted into the South Dakota Dynasty Trust.

The results were as follows:

    1) The home no longer "resides" on the financial statement of any individual family members.

    2) The home is totally removed from all heir's taxable estate (in perpetuity).

    3) The home is outside the claims of creditors (of all family members).

    4) The home is divorce proof (SD has a "floating spouse" rule that removes a spouse from any claims to an asset).

    5) No one ever has to lie to the IRS on the Form 1040 or 706 Tax Returns.

We created Argonne Trust Company, to help families restructure the title of their foreign home into a South Dakota trust and eliminate the potential ownership problems.

Why Buy Life Insurance in South Dakota

The State Premium Tax

Why is it that US companies are manufacturing their products in China? Simply because they can do it more cheaply than in the states?

And so it is with life insurance. One of the "raw materials" that go into manufacturing a policy is the state premium tax. South Dakota has the lowest premium insurance rate of any state. South Dakota's insurance premium tax rate is 8 basis points and both New York and Delaware's are 200. Hence, if you could purchase your life insurance through a SD ILIT, it may be possible (and certainly in the Private Placement Life Insurance arena) to manufacture your life insurance in a more cost efficient way.

10-44-2. (1) (a) Two and one-half percent of premiums for a **life policy** on the first one hundred thousand dollars of annual premium, and eight one-hundredths of a percent for that portion of a policy's annual life premiums exceeding one hundred thousand dollars;

(Life Insurance = 2.5% on $100,000 and .08% thereafter)

(b) One and one-fourth percent of the consideration for an **annuity** contract on the first five hundred thousand dollars of consideration, and eight one-hundredths of a percent for that portion of the consideration on an annuity contract exceeding five hundred thousand dollars;

(Annuity = 1.25% on $500,000 and .08% thereafter)

The South Dakota Advantage							
Life Insurance Premium $ 10,000,000							
	First $100,000		Above $100,000		Total State Premium Tax	
State Premium Tax in New York	200 bps	$2,000	200 bps	$ 198,000	$	200,000
State Premium Tax in South Dakota	250 bps	$ 2,500	8 bps	$ 79,200	$	81,700
Tax Savings by utilizing Argonne Trust Company, South Dakota					$ 118,300	

ARGONNE TRUST COMPANY

Obviously, the larger the policy size the greater the premium tax savings.

STATE PREMIUM TAX RATES

STATE	Insurance Premium Tax	STATE	Insurance Premium Tax
South Dakota	8 bps	South Dakota	8 bps
Alabama	230 bps	Missoiuri	200 bps
Alaska	10 bps	Montana	275 bps
Arizona	200 bps	Nebraska	350 bps
Arkansas	250 bps	Nevada	350 bps
California	235 bps	New Hampshire	100 bps
Colorado	200 bps	New Jersey	210 bps
Connecticut	175 bps	New Mexico	300 bps
District of Columbia	170 bps	New York	200 bps
Delaware	200 bps	North Carolina	190 bps
Florida	175 bps	North Dakota	200 bps
Georgia	275 bps	Ohio	140 bps
Hawaii	275 bps	Oklahoma	225 bps
Idaho	230 bps	Oregon	200 bps
Illinois	50 bps	Pennsylvania	200 bps
Indiana	175 bps	Rhode Island	200 bps
Iowa	100 bps	South Carolina	75 bps
Kansas	200 bps	Tennessee	175 bps
Kentucky	200 bps	Texas	175 bps
Louisiana	225 bps	Utah	225 bps
Maine	200 bps	Vermont	200 bps
Maryland	200 bps	Virginia	225 bps
Massachuetts	200 bps	Washington	200 bps
Michigan	200 bps	West Virginia	200 bps
Minnesota	200 bps	Wisconsin	200 bps
Mississippi	300 BPS	Wyoming	75 bps

Private Placement Life Insurance

The sophisticated investor can benefit by employing the life insurance policy of the VUL contract to his or her Registered Investment Advisory investments in a manner that can promote a significantly higher net "after-tax" return on investment. The concept of Private Placement Life Insurance (PPLI) is a relatively new development in the world of Insurance Dedicated Funds (IDF) for the Registered Investment Advisors (RIA). However, it is not difficult to understand that if there is a way to structure a particular investment within a tax advantaged life insurance policy; the fund's regular investors will be much better served on a total return basis.

The PPLI incorporates RIA investment strategies into its chassis which become the policy's cash values. The policies are designed to provide a sufficient amount of insurance death benefit in order to comply with the requirements of the United States Internal Revenue Code definition of life insurance (IRC Sec 7702) (as opposed to characterization as an investment policy or annuity) and to provide a minimal increase in the actual death benefit in excess of the cash value account accumulation.

The chart found on page 34 depicts an example of such a policy design and affords a simple contrast to that of a taxable investment.

In the following example, we have assumed a healthy, non-smoker 50-year old male investing $10 million in an investment earning 8% per year after management fees. The marginal tax rate is assumed to be 47% (federal, state and local). The policy is a modified endowment contract ("MEC"), which uses the guideline premium/cash value corridor definition of life insurance.

This investment is compared to a similar deposit into a hypothetical PPLI policy. As the chart indicates, the cost of the "tax advantaged" IDF is substantially lower than the cost of paying income taxes.

The illustrated results project a total cost of 138 basis points in the early years dropping to approximately 80 basis points over time as the "price tag" to avoid income tax. Among items that may affect this illustration are the actual age and health of the insured, investor's actual marginal tax rate and the actual performance of the IDF.

Male Age 50 - $10.0 Million

HYPOTHETICAL ILLUSTRATION

Year	Net Taxable Investment Value	End of Year Policy Cash Value	Death Benefit	Net Taxable Investment IRR	Policy Cash Value IRR	Death Benefit IRR
1	10,795,000	11,362,510	35,943,930	7.95%	13.62%	259.44%
2	11,653,203	12,912,620	35,943,930	7.95%	13.62%	89.60%
3	12,579,632	14,684,290	35,943,930	7.95%	13.65%	53.18%
4	13,579,713	16,710,230	35,943,930	7.95%	13.69%	37.68%
5	14,659,300	19,019,330	35,943,930	7.95%	13.75%	29.15%
10	21,489,508	36,525,140	48,943,680	7.95%	13.84%	17.24%
15	31,502,114	70,617,360	86,153,180	7.95%	13.91%	15.44%
20	46,179,894	136,575,200	158,427,200	7.95%	13.95%	14.82%
30	99,238,319	525,828,200	552,119,600	7.95%	14.13%	14.32%
40	213,258,263	2,004,725,000	2,104,961,000	7.95%	14.17%	14.31%

At the death of the insured, the insurer will pay out the policy death benefit income tax free (which includes the value of the insurance dedicated fund account) to the beneficiary designated by the owner of the policy. During the life of the insured, the policy can be cashed in for an amount equal to the value of the insurance dedicated fund (IDF) without the imposition of surrender charges (that would normally apply in a traditional life insurance policy), or the owner of the policy may access cash value via the use of loans taken against the policy.

The cash value of the PPLI policy is increased by the investment performance and yields on the IDF managed account assets, without any erosion for income taxes. The cost of setting up this type of policy (including issuance costs, servicing fees, etc.) will generally be significantly less than the first year's income tax savings on the IDF returns.

Annual charges, excluding the cost of the insurance protection, will be between 85 and 125 basis points. In return for the willingness to

[34]

assume these costs, the policy owner and the beneficiaries will not be subject to current taxation of the inside build-up of the policy cash value (the separately managed investment fund value and accumulated earnings). Moreover, if the policy is maintained until the death of the insured, the entire death benefit will be received by the beneficiary free of all U.S. income taxes, including all of the earnings from the IDF from inception of the policy.

Estate Planning with PPLI

If the ownership of the policy is properly structured and the insured has no control over the policy or incidents of ownership, the policy death benefit will be exempt from the federal estate tax. The net benefit of sheltering the investment income and accumulations from income and estate tax is the equivalent of a 400% + incremental rate of return (in any given year) on investment vis-à-vis the ownership of income and estate taxable investments. The compounding effect of this incremental advantage produces much larger advantages over time.

As a part of the estate planning process, PPLI offering policy investment options may prove to be the appropriate solution to help meet a variety of objectives. PPLI is effectively an institutionally priced or "no-load" life insurance policy with very sophisticated investment options.

Tax Free Exchanges (Sec. 1035) to PPLI

For those wealthy individual investors who currently have traditional cash value life insurance policies (whole life or universal life), the possibility of securing a more aggressive investment alternative and a lower cost structure for their life insurance may be available. These existing policies may be exchanged for new policies without the imposition of income tax on the accumulated earnings within the policy. The Internal Revenue Code enables owners of such policies the opportunity to exchange them for new policies on an income tax-free basis provided that the rules of Section 1035 and the individual State regulations are complied with. Section 1035 provides that an existing insurance policy may be exchanged for a new insurance policy on the same insured providing all of the Federal and State formalities attendant to the exchange are completed between the insurance companies involved with the exchange.

These rules enable the exchange to occur with no cash coming into the hands of the policy owner at any time during the process. For example, it may, therefore, be possible for the wealthy investor with significant existing cash value life insurance that is owned in an irrevocable life insurance trust to seek the cooperation of the trustees of that trust in converting the existing policies into insurance policies that will provide enhanced benefits to family members. It is very important to note that these trusts may be useful in providing the beneficiaries with income and support benefits during the life of the insured patriarch or matriarch. However, the insured is subject to medical underwriting requirements. The existing policy should not be exchanged until the new insurance offer is in place.

One of the failures of traditional life insurance trust planning is that there is generally limited availability of funds to provide lifetime benefits because of the cost structure, and investment performance. It is not uncommon for the grantor/insured under such a trust to complain that there are no benefits available for their children "until I die".

PPLI with its potentially superior investment performance and lower cost structure is uniquely suited to meet the income needs of this grantor by enabling more aggressive investments that may increase cash accumulations which can be accessed as policy loans during their lifetime without compromising the integrity of the death benefits which the policy is designed to produce.

Purposeful Trusts

For quite some time I have wondered why so many individuals would postpone or avoid doing rather basic estate planning. Obviously, they knew that they were not going to live forever and that "the train wreck is coming." Yet they could not formalize and finalize their plans so that the proper legal instruments could be crafted and executed.

It was not until I began doing "values based planning" that the lightbulb went off. Traditional wealth management and estate planning revolves around "the person" – the beneficiary(ies). While 3 Dimensional Wealth™ management and estate planning revolves around "one's values" – the valu-ficiary(ies)™.

Listen in on the conversations that are typical for the procrastinator. *"I am worried about my daughter's marriage and don't want to complicate things right now."* *I don't know where my children will be settling down, so I'm going to put a hold on things."* *"I'm worried about the way my kids are spending money and I'm not sure that I want to give them anything until they get straightened out."* *"I haven't spoken to my son in ten years and I'm considering not leaving him a penny."* *"I have three kids and I want to treat them all equally but they are in such different places in their lives, so I have no idea how to balance things out."* *"I don't have any idea how much I should leave my children and grandchildren as I don't want to take away any incentive for them to be productive."* Do these sound familiar? Perhaps this is YOU?

What I noticed in each sentence of every conversation with a procrastinator was that the noun (a "natural life" or person) was the common denominator. And the common thread with every person/beneficiary is that life is unstable, at best. Hence, how then can one accurately hit the bullseye when the target is moving? It's like building a house upon the sand. Logically, it makes no sense, yet the whole estate planning paradigm is based on this premise.

Doomed for failure by design.

Promoting procrastination by default!

Contrast this to a 3 Dimensional Wealth™ plan; one that is values centric. Here the noun in the conversation is replaced, generating a very different result. *"I believe in providing for the best possible college education for my grandchildren."* *"I would like to provide the resources so that a mother could be a "stay at home mom" with her infant."* *"In order to promote a positive self-image for my heirs, we would like to provide the resources for engaging in active philanthropy."* *"It is our hope that family unity will be an ongoing priority for generations to come, and to that end we will provide funding for bi-annual family retreats."* *"Managing money (budgeting/debt management/investing) requires education and training hence, it is my desire to provide funding for a financial literacy course every 3 years for each adult heir over the age of 16."* *"In an effort learn to better communicate within our family, learn from each other (especially our elders) and promote our wonderful family heritage, I will fund a family values website as the central repository* for our family history." "In our fast-paced world (and getting faster with each generation), we have established a "family retreat" (ski home) where a large number of our family can gather together for respite." If these statements are truly based upon one's family values, they will stand the test of time. They will remain true for generations and they can be the "valu-ficiaries™" for one's estate planning. This is like the man who built his house upon the rock. No need to procrastinate, as long as you know and can articulate your values.

Bottom line: Basing your estate planning on your beneficiaries' situation is like building a house on sand. Basing your estate planning on your valu-ficiaries™ is like building a house on rock.

This new perspective is the most radical change in the world of planning which requires shedding your old preconceived notions of what planning is and embracing the transformational values based approach of 3 Dimensional Wealth™.

Finally, no need to procrastinate any longer! But values based planning requires a process to get you from thought to finish. At 3 Dimensional Wealth Advisory, we have a four step approach that to do just that;

- Identifies your dominant values,
- Prioritizes your values,
- Creates values base trust language, and
- Completes the program with ongoing administration.

Never before has any one firm "connected the dots" to help you create, protect and preserve both your values and your valuables in perpetuity!

Note: *Valu-ficiary is the desired principle (value) to be perpetuated through the distribution of financial wealth for the ultimate benefit of heirs.*

A purposeful trust is a type of trust which has <u>no named beneficiaries,</u> but instead exists for advancing some non-charitable purpose of some kind. In most jurisdictions, such trusts are not enforceable outside of certain limited and anomalous exceptions, but some countries

[38]

(Bermuda, Isle of Man, and the Virgin Islands) along with South Dakota have enacted legislation specifically to promote the use of non-charitable purpose trusts.

A purposeful trust provides an opportunity to put one's personal fingerprint and voice on the document in a personalized way. It speaks to beneficiaries on an individual basis and is a vehicle to combat the negative psychological implications of "I didn't trust you." It is designed to give beneficiaries great opportunity and hope. It affords the opportunity for a family **to perpetuate its values, in perpetuity**.

The emphasis of a purposeful trust is to truly make the document clear, and more readable. This is the most effective way for the trust creator's purpose and intent to be revealed. It illustrates one's beneficial reflections and life experiences, providing beneficiaries with words of wisdom.

A purposeful trust is not an incentive trust which requires "acceptable" behavior for receiving trust benefits. These provisions have caused antagonistic feelings towards the grantor and trustees. In today's society, self-absorbed thinking and actions dominate the landscape. The goal of a purposeful trust is to provide the beneficiaries a platform for expressing appreciation and gratitude for what they receive. This is accomplished by capturing the meaning behind the gifts provided in the trust. In addition, the symbolic power of the naming of the trust can create positive emotions for both the grantor and the beneficiaries.

Finally, a purposeful trust, hopefully, will turn the planning process into a fun experience. The results of completing such a trust will project the grantor's life into the lives of the beneficiaries for generations.

Decanting

The "Do Over" Trust: Decanting to SD

After an irrevocable trust is established, grantors often change their minds or the circumstances change that cause the client to want to change the provisions of the trust. These might include;

- Extending the terms of the trust
- Changing support trusts into discretionary trusts

- Correcting drafting errors or ambiguous terms
- Changing the governing laws of the trust
- Modifying powers of appointment
- Changing trustee provisions
- Combining trusts for greater efficiency
- Separating trusts
- Creating special a special needs trust
- Qualifying a trust to own Sub S stock

The answer is to decant the trust. By this we mean transferring assets from an existing irrevocable trust to a new or another existing irrevocable trust, which may have a different term.

South Dakota is one of the 22 states having adopted decanting statues. In addition, this jurisdiction does not require the trustee to notify the beneficiaries of the trustee's intent to decant trust assets to a new receiving trust!

In summary:

South Dakota does allow you to decant a discretionary trust.

South Dakota does allow you to decant a trust with an ascertainable standard (such as health, education, maintenance and support).

South Dakota does allow you to decant a trust with an ascertainable standard into a discretionary trust.

South Dakota does allow you to remove a mandatory income interest.

South Dakota does NOT require notice to be sent to all beneficiaries.

South Dakota does allow the second trust to give a power of appointment to someone that can be exercised in favor of someone who isn't a beneficiary of the first trust.

Once again, Steve Oshins in his annual rankings, has placed South Dakota in the #1 position with regards to decanting.

3rd Annual Trust Decanting State Rankings Chart

Rank	State	Has Decanting Statute? (60% weight)	Can Decant Trust with Ascert. Stand? (7.5% weight)	Notice to Beneficiaries Required? (7.5% weight)	Can Decant Trust with Ascertainable Standard into Discretionary Trust? (7.5% weight)	Can Remove Mandatory Income Interest? (2.5% weight)	Allow Power of Appointment in Second Trust to Bene fbo Non-Bene's? (2.5% weight)	Can Accelerate Remainder Bene's Interest? (2.5% weight)	Dynasty Trust State Ranking (7.5% weight)	Domestic Asset Protection Trust State Ranking (2.5% weight)	Total Score
1	SD	55-2-15-21	Yes	No	Yes	Yes	Yes	Yes	Ranked #1	Ranked #2	99.5
2	NV	163.556, Sec. 57	Yes	No	Yes	Yes	Yes	Yes	Ranked #2	Ranked #1	99
3	TN	35-15-816(b)(27)	Yes	Yes	No	Yes	No	Yes	Ranked #3	Ranked #3	93
4	NH	564-B:4-418	Yes	No, except charitable trusts	Yes	No	Yes	Silent	Ranked #8	Ranked #10	91
5	DE	12-3528	Yes	No	No	Yes	Yes	No	Ranked #6 (tie)	Ranked #5 (tie)	87
6	OH	5808.18	Yes	Yes	No	Yes	Yes	No	Ranked #6 (tie)	Ranked #4	80
7 (tie)	AK	13.36.157-159; 13.36.215	Yes	Yes	No, except after first trust would have ended	No	Yes	No	Ranked #4	Ranked #7	77.5
7 (tie)	IL	760 ILCS 5/16.4	Yes	Yes	No	No	Yes	Silent	Ranked #9	Not allowed	77.5
9	IN	30-4-3-36	Yes	Yes	Yes	No	Silent	Silent	Unranked	Not allowed	75
10 (tie)	MO	456.4-419	Yes	Yes, only to beneficiaries of second trust	No	Yes	Silent	Yes	Unranked	Ranked #5 (tie)	74.5
10 (tie)	WY	4-10-816(xxviii) (very short)	Yes	No	Yes	Silent	Silent	Silent	Ranked #5	Ranked #8	74.5
12 (tie)	SC	62-7-816A	Yes	Yes	No	Yes	Yes	No	Unranked	Not allowed	72.5
12 (tie)	TX	112.071 to 112.087	Yes	Yes	No	No	Yes	Yes	Unranked	Not allowed	72.5
14	VA	64.2-778.1	Yes	Yes	No, except if court approval	No	Yes	No	Unranked	Ranked #13	70.5
15 (tie)	KY	386.175	Yes	Yes	No	No	Yes	No	Unranked	Not allowed	70
15 (tie)	NC	36C-8-816.1	Yes	Yes	No	No	Yes	No	Unranked	Not allowed	70
17	RI	18-4-31	Yes	Yes	Silent	No	Silent	No	Unranked	Ranked #9	68.5
18 (tie)	AZ	14-10819 (short)	Yes	No	Yes	No	Silent	Silent	Unranked	Not allowed	67.5
18 (tie)	MI	5799.7820x / 5556.125a	No	Yes	Yes	No	Yes	Silent	Unranked	Not allowed	67.5
18 (tie)	MN	502.851	Yes	Yes	No, except after first trust would have ended	No	No	No	Unranked	Not allowed	67.5
18 (tie)	NY	10-6.6	Yes	Yes	No	No	No	No	Unranked	Not allowed	67.5
18 (tie)	WI	701.0418	Yes	Yes	Yes	No	Silent	No	Unranked	Not allowed	67.5
23	FL	736.04117	No	Yes	No	No	Silent	Silent	Ranked #10	Not allowed	63.5

A trust can be moved to a different jurisdiction through one of three methods; modification, reformation or decant. The chart that follows is designed to illustrate the differences.

	MODIFICATION		REFORMATION	DECANT
What is your Outcome Criteria?	#1 - To become a Directed Trust (including a Trust Protector with Investment & Distribution Committees.)	#1 - To become a Directed Trust (including a Trust Protector with Investment & Distribution Committees.)	#1 - To become a Directed Trust (including a Trust Protector with Investment & Distribution Committees.)	#1 - To become a Directed Trust (including a Trust Protector with Investment & Distribution Committees.)
			#2 - Change Despositive Provisions (thay may include values based	#2 - Modify powers of appointment to have general powers.
			#3 - Changing a support trust into a discretionalry trust (for better asset protection).	#3 - Changing a support trust into a discretionalry trust (for better asset protection).
				#4 - Extending the terms of the trust (to modify "birthday cake" distributions).
				#5 - Broaden discretion in making distribution of "distributable net Income."
Required Procedures	All beneficiaries must "sign off."	Court petition with signed order of approval.	Court petition with signed order of approval.	New trust is created and no court approval is required.
Dominant Benefit	Least expensive.	Beneficiaries cannot contest in the future.	Beneficiaries cannot contest in the future.	Beneficiaries do not need to be given notice of new trust.
Estimated Legal Fees	$1,500 - $2,000	$4,000	$4,000	$4,000
Timeframe to Complete	21 - 30 Days	21 - 30 Days	45 - 60 Days	60 - 75 Days

The Governor's Task Force

South Dakota takes seriously its position as a leader in the domestic trust arena. Hence, the establishment of the Governor's Task Force on Trust Administration Review and Reform. Each year the mission of this task force is to contrast and compare the various trust provisions that are deemed to be of utmost importance. It then proposes legislation (with the explicit purpose of being as good or better than any other jurisdiction within each category) for the state to enact. Each year if the bill is passed it goes into law on July 1st. This proactive task force is what will continue to make South Dakota rank at the very top of its peers.

South Dakota Exempt from ALL Taxes

South Dakota is a pure no trust income state and may be used in perpetuity since 1986.

The common law against perpetuities is not enforced in South Dakota. This means that a person can create a trust in South Dakota and avoid federal transfer tax system (gift and estate planning generation-skipping) forever, if a family chooses.

South Dakota does not impose any state taxation on the assets in a South Dakota trust. There are no capital gains, dividend interest nor intangible taxes.

South Dakota has neither estate nor inheritance tax. Contrast this to the chart below. This will highlight the states whose residents should be mindful of the additional trust planning that should be initiated.

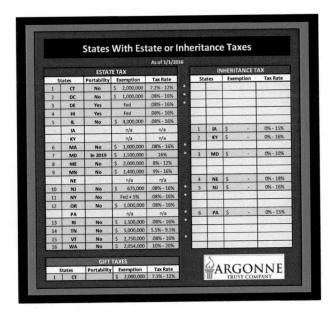

States With Estate or Inheritance Taxes

As of 1/1/2016

ESTATE TAX					INHERITANCE TAX			
	States	Portability	Exemption	Tax Rate		States	Exemption	Tax Rate
1	CT	No	$ 2,000,000	7.2% - 12%				
2	DC	No	$ 1,000,000	.08% - 16%				
3	DE	Yes	Fed	.08% - 16%				
4	HI	Yes	Fed	.08% - 16%				
5	IL	No	$ 4,000,000	.08% - 16%				
	IA		n/a	n/a	1	IA	$ -	0% - 15%
	KY		n/a	n/a	2	KY	$ -	0% - 16%
6	MA	No	$ 1,000,000	.08% - 16%				
7	MD	In 2019	$ 1,500,000	16%	3	MD	$ -	0% - 10%
8	ME	No	$ 2,000,000	8% - 12%				
9	MN	No	$ 1,400,000	9% - 16%				
	NE		n/a	n/a	4	NE	$ -	0% - 18%
10	NJ	No	$ 675,000	.08% - 16%	5	NJ	$ -	0% - 16%
11	NY	No	Fed + 5%	.08% - 16%				
12	OR	No	$ 1,000,000	.08% - 16%				
	PA		n/a	n/a	6	PA	$ -	0% - 15%
13	RI	No	$ 1,500,000	.08% - 16%				
14	TN	No	$ 5,000,000	5.5% - 9.5%				
15	VT	No	$ 2,750,000	.08% - 16%				
16	WA	No	$ 2,054,000	10% - 20%				

GIFT TAXES				
	States	Portability	Exemption	Tax Rate
1	CT		$ 2,000,000	7.5% - 12%

ARGONNE
TRUST COMPANY

South Dakota – The One And Only

So how then would one determine where to situs one's trust? It all comes down to which state can accommodate one's desires. And the major categories that will determine your decision will be most likely these four;

- Provision for directed trusts,
- Provision for dynasty trusts (without income taxes),
- Provision for asset protection trusts, and
- Provision for purposeful trusts.

When crossed checked with the other states, only one state can achieve total satisfaction of obtaining 100% of the desired provisions.

Hence, Argonne Trust Company has made ourselves truly a "friendly" trust company so that the traditional barriers to entry will be eliminated.

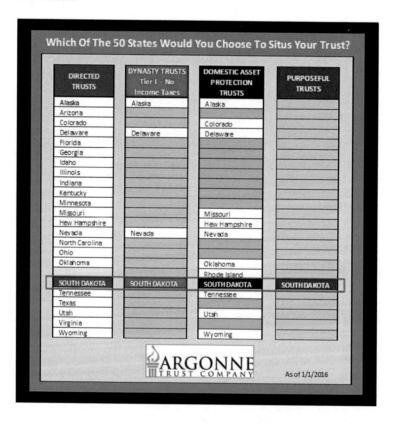

DIRECTED TRUSTS	DYNASTY TRUSTS Tier I – No Income Taxes	DOMESTIC ASSET PROTECTION TRUSTS	PURPOSEFUL TRUSTS
Alaska	Alaska	Alaska	
Arizona			
Colorado		Colorado	
Delaware	Delaware	Delaware	
Florida			
Georgia			
Idaho			
Illinois			
Indiana			
Kentucky			
Minnesota			
Missouri		Missouri	
Hew Hampshire		Hew Hampshire	
Nevada	Nevada	Nevada	
North Carolina			
Ohio			
Oklahoma		Oklahoma	
		Rhode Island	
SOUTH DAKOTA	SOUTH DAKOTA	SOUTH DAKOTA	SOUTH DAKOTA
Tennessee		Tennessee	
Texas			
Utah		Utah	
Virginia			
Wyoming		Wyoming	

Which Of The 50 States Would You Choose To Situs Your Trust?

ARGONNE TRUST COMPANY

As of 1/1/2016

Why Argonne Trust Company Over The Other SD Companies?

David vs. Goliath

Why would one ever think that a shepherd boy with a slingshot could take down a giant? But "little giants" do exist both then and now. Argonne Trust Company is an example of how small is better. Here's why:

Argonne Trust Company is one of the public trust companies in South Dakota. What is significant about this is that SD is considered the #1 state in the US for trust activity. So Argonne Trust's size does not stop it from providing all of the best trust provisions to its clients.

Let's talk about experience. Our seven Trust Marketing Officers have 199 years of collective experience in the financial services industry. The level of professional education is at a par with any trust company in America. In addition, our Chief Trust Officer has over 20 years of experience in trust administration.

How will one know that Argonne Trust Company will continue to be solvent? The South Dakota Division of Banking regulates the activities of all its trust companies. Argonne Trust Company must maintain ample reserves to comply with the requirements along with mandatory D&O insurance. In addition to the Division of Banking's supervision, Argonne Trust Company is subject to an independent audit. In other words, Argonne Trust Company plays by the same rules as "the big boys" and has the wherewithal to handle trusts of any size.

Large trust companies would like you to think it is "safer" to place assets under their custody. Please be advised that Argonne Trust Company does not take custody of any of its client's assets. All assets reside within one of our institutional investment platforms including Fidelity, Schwab and TD Ameritrade. These custodians have billions of dollars under management and rival, if not exceed, the assets under management of the large trust companies.

How about personal service? With Argonne "Boutique" Trust Company you have your own personal Trust Marketing Officer. These individuals are providing the stability that you would want for your family. How often have you dealt with large organizations where you have never met the individuals with whom you speak or never deal with the same officer from year to year? What about knowledge about your family? Argonne's close ties to its clients make it easier to make discretionary distributions to the beneficiaries in accordance with the grantor's wishes. In addition, by operating as a "directed" trust, a close working relationship between one's Trust Marketing Officer and the family's Investment and Distribution Committees is paramount. This aspect of the day to day operations of the trust makes Argonne Trust Company the natural choice.

Would you be surprised to learn that Argonne Trust Company's fees fall at the lower end of the spectrum? Without the overhead that the larger trust companies must maintain, Argonne can pass on these savings to its clients.

Perhaps you might think that a small company would be lacking in the area of technology. Think again. Did you know that Argonne Trust Company operates on the Business Process Management software platform Megethos[3]? This software earned Diefendorf Capital the 2010 Gold Medal for North America, Central America and South America from the Gartner organization. You might recognize some of the other winners; Accenture, Nikon, Tractor-Caterpillar and the US Air Force.

Other trust companies compete by primarily selling the tax savings of a trust which aids in increasing a family's assets. Argonne Trust Company not only seeks to preserve ones "valuables" through these traditional weapons but also understands the importance of perpetuating a family's "values" to produce well-adjusted and productive heirs. This unique values based planning is like providing "David" with nuclear weapons.

Pound for pound, Argonne Trust Company has all of the tools to provide one's family with an outstanding trust experience. With offices in Locust Valley (Long Island), NY, Park Avenue, NYC, Charlotte, NC, Dallas, TX and Sioux Falls, SD.

The Purposeful "Values Based" Trust

A purposeful trust is **THE** vehicle that allows grantors to define one's values and put one's personal fingerprint and voice on the document in a personalized way. It speaks to beneficiaries on an individual basis.

The goal of a purposeful trust is to provide the beneficiaries a platform for expressing appreciation and gratitude for what they receive. This is accomplished by capturing the meaning behind the gifts provided in the trust. In addition, the symbolic power of the naming of the trust can create positive emotions for both the grantor and the beneficiaries.

We have created a process that will be the roadmap for virtually everyone to follow and achieve values based planning.

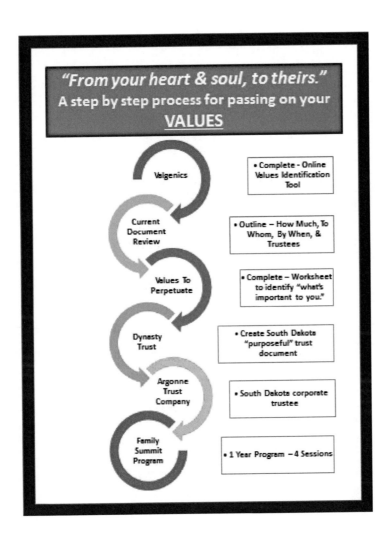

A Discussion About Fees

How A Trust Company Earns Its Fees

The trustee is the person or corporate entity that manages the trust's affairs in order to ensure that it achieves the goals set by its creators. Trust administration issues, deadlines and procedures can strangle otherwise financially sophisticated people in red tape.

This is a <u>fiduciary role</u>, and as such the penalties for failure are clear-cut and severe. Your clients already know what you do to manage their money, but the trustee relationship is likely to be new and somewhat outside their experience.

Because you will want to remain the primary point of contact between clients and the trust company, you must have a basic understanding of the primary duties of the corporate trustee and any trust officers assigned to your clients' accounts.

<u>Non-discretionary tasks are not optional</u>. These include making income payments monthly, quarterly, annually or as otherwise directed by the trust. Trustees must also pay out principal as set forth in the trust and attend to all other matters the trust directs. Tax and other filing deadlines must be met in full. Any additional duties or instructions explicitly called for in the trust documents must be carried out.

<u>Discretionary tasks give the trustee more room for personal interpretation</u>. If the trust is silent on an issue, the trustee's fiduciary duty may require him or her to make discretionary decisions. For example, a trust may indicate that the trustee can make principal payments "after considering other sources of income available to the beneficiary," in which case the trustee should demand extensive documentation from the beneficiary before making a decision.

Many trust officers also perform miscellaneous activities on behalf of the beneficiaries as part of their overall ethic of service, even if these tasks are not explicitly mandated in the trust itself.

By Melani Shanks, First Foundation

ADD UP THE COSTS

Naturally, corporate trustees need to charge for their service. While regulators are pushing for greater transparency here, this fee is often all-inclusive or bundled in such a way that beneficiaries and their advisors have a hard time determining where their money goes.

Traditional all-in-one trust companies further obscured the cash flows by charging a fee that compensates them for their investment management services, fiduciary risk and other "soft non-value-added services" provided to clients.

Directed trusts, on the other hand, generally separate the investment advisory fee from the corporate trustee fee. As a result, clients receive much clearer insight into what they are paying -and often a lower total fee as well.

In general, <u>fee schedules for directed trust</u> companies fall in a range from 0.50% to 0.75% on the first $1 million and then drop according to varying breakpoints thereafter. Minimum annual fees range from $4,000 regardless of asset level, although some types of trust start in the $1,500 range. A few vendors will charge a flat fee for any amount of assets.

<u>Additional fees may apply</u> for real estate held in trust, estate settlement, termination, tax preparation and/or filing, or miscellaneous extraordinary services.

Note: The IRS has ruled that all corporate trustees are required to separately account for investment and administration fees. This is intended to remove the tax advantage of a "unitary" trust in which the entire trustee fee can be deducted, as opposed to a trust that charges separate fees and only allows partial deductibility of fees. Directed trusts already break out the fees in this way, but because this is a relatively new development, it gives you a good "talking point" in your negotiations with trust companies.

By Christopher J. McCutcheon, Private Trust Co.

A corporate trustee in the State of South Dakota

Potential clients for our trust company have asked their advisers (CPAs & attorneys) to review our proposal for establishing and administering their Dynasty Trust. I have heard these exact words said, *"That fee seems awfully high, they really don't do anything after the first year. I'm named trustee on a client's trust and I don't do anything."*

I too, am named trustee on a few client's NY trust and I too, do nothing. But being a corporate trustee in SD is a significantly different animal. Here's why:

1) As a corporate trust company, we come under the jurisdiction of the Division of Banking in the State of South Dakota. The requirements for obtaining and maintaining your trust charter are extensive. And as part of the ongoing process, we are subject to a 2 week audit ($25,000 that we pay to the Division of Banking for their field work) to review each and every trust in our portfolio.

2) The Division of Banking requires us to maintain a $500,000 of capital on deposit as a reserve, with an additional $1,500,000 available, if necessary, to cover potential liability exposure.

3) The Division requires $1,000,000 of D&O coverage for our 7 trust marketing officers and 1 chief trust officers.

4) An independent audit is also required annually in preparation for the Division of Banking's audit.

5) We must adhere to the 136 page Trust Policy Manual covering 65 sections of the law.

6) In order to have your trust to receive the benefits of South Dakota law, we must maintain an office (currently in Sioux Falls, SD) along with 2 employees to handle the fiduciary work.

7) We are required to pay an asset based tax to the Division of Banking in South Dakota based on the value of your trust.

8) The Division of Banking requires that two of our board meetings be held in South Dakota to maintain our SD situs for your trust.

9) All of our Trust Marketing Officers must be Registered Fiduciaries, and operate under the guidelines for fiduciaries.

All of these requirements are necessary for you to have a trust in South Dakota. (And let me just say that all trusts are not created equal. There are numerous distinctions between a NY trust and a SD trust. So if you are told, *"we'll just do a NY trust, it's simpler,"* you are losing significant benefits afforded through SD.)

The following requirements are necessary to run the day to day, month to month fiduciary operations of your trust.

10) Our trust company not only acts as the administrative trustee, but is a member of the investment committee and distribution committee.

11) We are required to review each trust monthly at our board meetings and keep the minutes (even if there is a "no action").

12) We must maintain a trust money market account which will receive trust income and contributions and from which trust expenditures and distributions will be disbursed.

13) We handle required / discretionary distributions pursuant to the trust's terms.

14) We must maintain storage of tangible personalty and evidence of intangible trust property (i.e. certificates of LLCs).

15) We must maintain trust records and submit them to the regulators at each audit.

16) We originate, facilitate and review trust accountings, reports and other communications with the grantor and trustees, beneficiaries and unrelated third parties.

17) We respond to inquiries from the grantor, and trustees, beneficiaries and third parties concerning any trust created hereunder.

18) We execute documents (at the direction of the Investment Committee) with respect to trust investment transactions.

19) We make payment on installment obligations, if required (one payment – interest and/or principal- annually per obligation).

20) Preparation of fiduciary tax return is included as part of the ATC fee.

So having said all of that, ATC charges on three levels;

- a subscription fee (one time) to establish the trust in SD,

- a base annual fee (for maintaining the trust situs in SD), and
- an annual fiduciary fee (for the running of the plan in SD and preparing the fiduciary trust tax return).

Breaking Down The Fees

Subscription Fees:

1st Entitiy Established Within The Trust	$	1,500.00
Each additional Entitiy Within The Trust	$	500.00

Establishing a trust in SD requires that the assets within the trust are registered on our administrative platform. Each asset added to the trust, adds another layer of complexity.

Annual Base Fee:

1st Entitiy Established Within The Trust	$	4,500.00
Each additional Entitiy Within The Trust	$	1,000.00

The base fee covers mandatory requirements for operating a trust company in SD. These include;

1) Annual Audit by the SD Banking Division by Trust
2) Annual Trust Review by Independent Auditor
3) Mandatory reserve requirement - $500,000 + $1,500,000
4) Mandatory $1,000,000 E&O coverage for 9 employees/directors.
5) Quarterly trust meetings (with minutes) based on 136 page Trust Policy Manual
6) Mandatory office presence in SD.
7) Mandatory trust officers in SD.
8) Two mandatory board meetings in SD.
9) Trust tax return, and each additional entity adds another layer of complexity.

Fiduciary Fee:

Portfolio Asset Based	15 bps	Fully offset @ CPR
Real Estate Asset Based	20 bps	
Closely Held Asset Based	25 bps	

The fidicuary fee is derived by the services provided throughout the year. These fess are asset based depending upon the nature of the assets within the trust.

1) Each trust marketing office is a Registered Fiduciary and operate under its standards.
2) SD Division of Banking taxes each trust based upon the value of its assets.
3) Mandatory montlhy review of each trust (even if ther is a "no action")
4) Maintenance of the trust money market for contributions / distirubtions.
5) Handle required / discretionary distributions pursuant to the trust terms
6) Responding to inquires from the grantor, beneficiaries, can committee members
7) Execution of documents with respect to trust investment transactions.
8) Originate, facilitate and review trust accounting, with reporting on-line and in print.
9) Maintain storage of tangible personalty and evidence of intangible property (LLCs)

Argonne Trust Fee Schedule

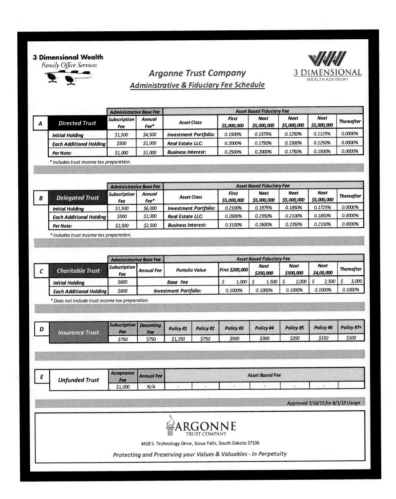

3 Dimensional Wealth
Family Office Services

Argonne Trust Company
Administrative & Fiduciary Fee Schedule

3 DIMENSIONAL
WEALTH ADVISORY

A	Directed Trust	Administrative Base Fee		Asset Based Fiduciary Fee					
		Subscription Fee	Annual Fee*	Asset Class	First $5,000,000	Next $5,000,000	Next $5,000,000	Next $5,000,000	Thereafter
	Initial Holding	$1,500	$4,500	Investment Portfolio:	0.1500%	0.1375%	0.1250%	0.1125%	0.0000%
	Each Additional Holding	$500	$1,000	Real Estate LLC:	0.2000%	0.1750%	0.1500%	0.1250%	0.0000%
	Per Note:	$1,000	$1,000	Business Interest:	0.2500%	0.2000%	0.1750%	0.1500%	0.0000%

* Includes trust income tax preparation.

B	Delegated Trust	Administrative Base Fee		Asset Based Fiduciary Fee					
		Subscription Fee	Annual Fee*	Asset Class	First $5,000,000	Next $5,000,000	Next $5,000,000	Next $5,000,000	Thereafter
	Initial Holding	$1,500	$6,000	Investment Portfolio:	0.2100%	0.1975%	0.1850%	0.1725%	0.0000%
	Each Additional Holding	$500	$1,000	Real Estate LLC:	0.2600%	0.2350%	0.2100%	0.1850%	0.0000%
	Per Note:	$2,500	$2,500	Business Interest:	0.3100%	0.2600%	0.2350%	0.2100%	0.0000%

* Includes trust income tax preparation.

C	Charitable Trust	Administrative Base Fee		Asset Based Fiduciary Fee					
		Subscription Fee	Annual Fee	Portolio Value	First $200,000	Next $250,000	Next $500,000	Next $4,00,000	Thereafter
	Initial Holding	$600		Base Fee	$ 1,000	$ 1,500	$ 2,000	$ 2,500	$ 3,000
	Each Additional Holding	$600		Investment Portfolio:	0.1000%	0.1000%	0.1000%	0.1000%	0.1000%

* Does not include trust income tax preparation.

D	Insurance Trust	Subscription Fee	Decanting Fee	Policy #1	Policy #2	Policy #3	Policy #4	Policy #5	Policy #6	Policy #7+
		$750	$750	$1,250	$750	$500	$300	$200	$150	$100

E	Unfunded Trust	Acceptance Fee	Annual Fee	Asset Based Fee					
		$1,000	N/A	-	-	-	-	-	-

Approved 7/16/15 for 8/1/15 Usage

ARGONNE
TRUST COMPANY

4418 S. Technology Drive, Sioux Falls, South Dakota 57106

Protecting and Preserving your Values & Valuables - In Perpetuity

Comparison of Fees

In summary, our fees are on average 30% less than our peers.

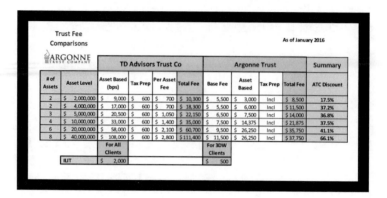

Trust Fee Comparisons — As of January 2016
ARGONNE TRUST COMPANY

# of Assets	Asset Level	TD Advisors Trust Co				Argonne Trust				Summary
		Asset Based Fee (bps)	Tax Prep	Per Asset Fee	Total Fee	Base Fee	Asset Based	Tax Prep	Total Fee	ATC Discount
2	$ 2,000,000	$ 9,000	$ 600	$ 700	$ 10,300	$ 5,500	$ 3,000	Incl	$ 8,500	17.5%
2	$ 4,000,000	$ 17,000	$ 600	$ 700	$ 18,300	$ 5,500	$ 6,000	Incl	$ 11,500	37.2%
3	$ 5,000,000	$ 20,500	$ 600	$ 1,050	$ 22,150	$ 6,500	$ 7,500	Incl	$ 14,000	36.8%
4	$ 10,000,000	$ 33,000	$ 600	$ 1,400	$ 35,000	$ 7,500	$ 14,375	Incl	$ 21,875	37.5%
6	$ 20,000,000	$ 58,000	$ 600	$ 2,100	$ 60,700	$ 9,500	$ 26,250	Incl	$ 35,750	41.1%
8	$ 40,000,000	$ 108,000	$ 600	$ 2,800	$ 111,400	$ 11,500	$ 26,250	Incl	$ 37,750	66.1%

	For All Clients			For 3DW Clients	
ILIT	$ 2,000			$ 500	

Review of Trustee Fees - 2016 — DIRECTED TRUSTEE FEES

Trust Company	State Charter	ILIT Fee	TRUST ASSETS					Tax Prep
			$ 1,000,000	$ 2,000,000	$ 3,000,000	$ 4,000,000	$ 5,000,000	
ARGONNE TRUST COMPANY	SD	$ 500	$ 6,000	$ 7,500	$ 9,000	$ 10,500	12,000	Incl
Advisory Trust Company of Delaware	DE		$ 5,000	$ 9,000	$ 14,000	$ 17,000	20,000	Not Incl
Alliance Trust Company	NV		$ 5,000	$ 9,500	$ 14,000	$ 19,500	23,500	Not Incl
BOK Financial Advisor Trust Services	Nat		$ 5,000	$ 9,000	$ 13,000	$ 16,500	20,000	Not Incl
Bryn Mawr Trust	DE		$ 6,000	$ 12,000	$ 18,000	$ 22,500	27,000	Not Incl
Comerica Bank & Trust Co	TX & Nat		$ 6,500	$ 12,300	$ 15,300	$ 20,300	25,300	Not Incl
Counsel Trust Company	PA		$ 4,000	$ 7,500	$ 11,000	$ 14,000	17,000	Not Incl
Cumberand Trust & Investment Co.	TN		$ 6,000	$ 12,000	$ 18,000	$ 24,000	30,000	Not Incl
Dunham Trust Company	NV & CO		$ 6,000	$ 11,000	$ 15,000	$ 19,000	23,000	Not Incl
Fiduciary Trust of New England	NH		$ 20,000	$ 20,000	$ 20,000	$ 20,000	20,000	Not Incl
First Foundation Bank	CA & NV		$ 10,000	$ -	$ -	$ -	-	Not Incl
First National Bank and Trust Company	Nat		$ 5,000	$ 9,000	$ 13,000	$ 17,000	20,000	Not Incl
Heritage Trust Company of New Mexico	NM		$ 5,000	$ 10,000	$ 15,000	$ 19,000	23,000	Not Incl
Independent Trust Company	SD		$ 7,500	$ 15,000	$ 22,500	$ 27,500	32,500	Not Incl
Kingdom Trust Company	SD		Self Directed IRAs					Not Incl
Midland State Bank	IL		$ 6,000	$ 11,000	$ 16,000	$ 20,500	25,000	Not Incl
National Advisors Trust Company	Nat		$ 4,500	$ 9,000	$ 13,000	$ 17,000	21,000	Not Incl
New York Private Trust	DE		$ 7,000	$ 7,000	$ 10,500	$ 14,000	17,500	Not Incl
Nevada Trust Company	NV	$ 750	$ 6,500	$ 12,000	$ 16,500	$ 21,000	25,400	Not Incl
Northern Trust Company	DE & IL		$ 20,000	$ 20,000	$ 20,000	$ 20,000	20,000	Not Incl
Prarie Financial Group	WI & IL		$ 4,500	$ 9,000	$ 13,500	$ 17,500	21,500	Not Incl
Premier Trust	NV		$ 6,000	$ 11,000	$ 14,500	$ 18,000	21,500	Not Incl
Principal Trust Company	DE							Not Incl
Provident Trust Group	NV		$ 5,500	$ 11,000	$ 16,500	$ 22,000	27,500	Not Incl
Sanat Fe Trust Company	NM		$ 7,500	$ 15,000	$ 22,500	$ 27,500	32,500	Not Incl
Saturna Trust Company	NV		$ 5,000	$ 10,000	$ 15,000	$ 20,000	25,000	Not Incl
Sterling Trustees, LLC	SD		Self Directed IRAs					Not Incl
Summit Trust Company	NV		$ 10,000	$ 18,000	$ 26,000	$ 33,000	40,000	Not Incl
TrustCorp America	DC		$ 5,000	$ 10,000	$ 15,000	$ 20,000	25,000	Not Incl
The Private Trust Company	Nat		$ 6,500	$ 12,000	$ 17,500	$ 22,000	26,500	$ 475
Wealth Advisors Trust Company	SD	$ 1,500	$ 6,000	$ 12,000	$ 17,000	$ 22,000	27,000	Not Incl
Wilmington Trust Corporation	DE		$ 6,000	$ 10,000	$ 14,000	$ 18,000	22,000	Not Incl
Zia Trust	NM		$ 10,000	$ 17,500	$ 22,500	$ 27,500	32,500	Not Incl
Reliance Trust Company of Delaware	DE & AZ, CA, FL, GA, TX, IL, RH, OR, PA	$ 1,500	$ 4,500	$ 9,000	$ 12,600	$ 16,200	19,800	Not Incl

ARGONNE TRUST COMPANY

Individual Trustee vs. Corporate Trustee

One of the barriers that grantors have to get over is the usage of a corporate trustee. In the past, an individual would simply name a close relative to accept the position of the ILIT's trustee. The idea was that there is nothing to do and I don't want to pay a fee. However, with the constant movement towards fiduciary responsibility and the liability that goes hand in hand, it is becoming more and more difficult to find individuals who will subject themselves to this precarious position.

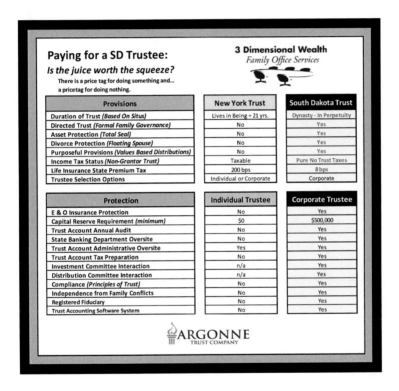

Paying for a SD Trustee:

Is the juice worth the squeeze?

There is a price tag for doing something and...
a pricetag for doing nothing.

3 Dimensional Wealth
Family Office Services

Provisions	New York Trust	South Dakota Trust
Duration of Trust *(Based On Situs)*	Lives in Being + 21 yrs.	Dynasty - In Perpetuity
Directed Trust *(Formal Family Governance)*	No	Yes
Asset Protection *(Total Seal)*	No	Yes
Divorce Protection *(Floating Spouse)*	No	Yes
Purposeful Provisions *(Values Based Distributions)*	No	Yes
Income Tax Status *(Non-Grantor Trust)*	Taxable	Pure No Trust Taxes
Life Insurance State Premium Tax	200 bps	8 bps
Trustee Selection Options	Individual or Corporate	Corporate

Protection	Individual Trustee	Corporate Trustee
E & O Insurance Protection	No	Yes
Capital Reserve Requirement *(minimum)*	$0	$500,000
Trust Account Annual Audit	No	Yes
State Banking Department Oversite	No	Yes
Trust Account Administrative Oversite	Yes	Yes
Trust Account Tax Preparation	No	Yes
Investment Committee Interaction	n/a	Yes
Distribution Committee Interaction	n/a	Yes
Compliance *(Principles of Trust)*	No	Yes
Independence from Family Conflicts	No	Yes
Registered Fiduciary	No	Yes
Trust Accounting Software System	No	Yes

ARGONNE TRUST COMPANY

Regardless of the benefits of a corporate trustee, in order to have a SD trust it is a requirement to utilize a SD chartered trust company to act as corporate trustee. Hence, we created Argonne Trust Company to act in this capacity, so that we can provide you will a full service (creation through to administration) program.

The following chart is a brief reminder of what can be accomplished in SD vs. NY (my state of residency). In fact, these two state jurisdictions have so little in common, that it would be an error in judgement to put them under the same "trust" umbrella. So since you do have a choice when selecting your trust situs, would you ever need to go beyond the borders of South Dakota?

STARTING WITH A BLANK PAGE
WHAT TRUST PROVISIONS WOULD YOU WANT?

The benefits of a SD trust justify the corporate trustee fees !	NY	SD
1 - Unlimited Trust Duration	NO	YES
Maximum years	90 - 110	Forever
2 - Directed Trust	NO	YES
Investment Committee	NO	YES
Distribution Committee	NO	YES
3 - Trust Protector *(12 powers)*	NO	YES
May modify trust	NO	YES
May terminate trust	NO	YES
May remove trustee	NO	YES
4 - Floating Spouse *(Divorce Protection)*	NO	YES
Including all heirs	NO	YES
5 - Asset Protection	-	-
Sole remedy charging order statute	NO	YES
Codifies the common law	NO	YES
Upholds Reinstatement 2nd	NO	YES
Negates Reinstatement 3rd	NO	YES
Negates Uniform Trust Code *(UTC)*	NO	YES
Privacy Protection *(Total Seal)*	NO	YES
Statute of Limitations	4 Yrs	2 Yrs
6 - Special Purpose Entities	NO	YES
7 - Preservation of Family Values	NO	YES

ARGONNE
TRUST COMPANY

Conclusion

Based upon the evidence provided in this booklet, I would submit that the jurisdiction of South Dakota is the best location for you to establish a Directed, Asset Protected, Dynasty, Purposeful (Values Based) Trust.

We at Argonne Trust Company have a unique value proposition by having pioneered the "Values Based" trusts in SD. In addition, we continue to explore what it is that clients are asking for and seeking to provide meaningful solutions that "scratch where they itch." Below is a chart that will give you a flavor for what relational and developmental concerns that we are seeking to address though values based trust distributions.

It is my hope that this is a work in process and that over the years we will hone our skills to help you capture, protect and preserve your values and valuables – in perpetuity.

Appendix

A: ATC Document Preparation Form

Document Preparation Information Sheet

Official Business Name:

Argonne Trust Company, Inc.

Mailing Address:

4418 S. Technology Drive

Sioux Falls, SD 57106

Telephone:

(877-3D-Wealth)

E-Mail:

Info@ArgonneTrust.com

Trust Marketing Officers:

Monroe Diefendorf, Jr.

Thomas Palumbo

Jeffrey Higgs

Steven Howe

David Taylor

Demetri Doumas

www.ArgonneTrust.com

3 DIMENSIONAL
WEALTH ADVISORY

1 | Page

[58]

Trust Personnel

Trust Name: _____
(this name should reflect the purpose of the trust)

Trust Grantor: _____
(this individual is making the initial gift into the trust)

Trust Protector: _____
(this individual may NOT be a family member or a business associate but a trusted advisor)

Investment Committee: _____

_____

_____

_____

(this can be made up of a Registered Investment Advisor and/or family members)

Distribution Committee: _____

_____

_____

_____

(this can be made up of Argonne Trust Company and/or a trusted advisor, however, not a beneficiary)

[59]

Trust Beneficiaries

a. Discretionary Beneficiaries *(by Name with Date of Birth):*_____

_____

_____

b. HEMS (Health, Education, Maintenance, Support) Beneficiaries *(by class)*

_____

_____

_____

c. Values Based Distributions *(by purpose) – see attached samples*

    i. Family: _____

    _____

    ii. Education: _____

    _____

    iii. Financial: _____

    _____

    iv. Philanthropic: _____

    _____

    v. Spiritual: _____

    _____

    vi. Health: _____

    _____

vii. Unique Value Provision: _____
_____

d. Default Final Beneficiary *(by organization name)*
_____
_____

e. Miscellaneous Notes
_____
_____
_____
_____
_____
_____
_____

3 Dimensional Wealth
Family Office Services

Attachment

Values Based Distributions

Perpetuating your Values In Perpetuity

Valgenics as an Asset Class	Possible Distribution Options for Valgenics Categories
Family	
1	Home Court Advantage: Purchase / Support of a Family Compound
2	Family Unity: Annual / Bi-Annual Reunions
3	Marriage Encouragement / Maintenance: Counseling & Retreats, Wedding Participation - 25%
4	Child Rearing: Subsidy for Stay @ Home Mom;
5	Personal Histories: Written manuscripts, DVD, etc
Health	
1	Extraordinary Life Support: Subsidy for Medical Procedures
2	Physical Well Being: Funding for gym memberships, addiction programs, weight management
3	Medical Insurance: COBRA subsidy if unemployed (and searching for employment)
4	Sports Participation: Funding for pre-college extra-curricular sports fees
5	Competitive Sports Participation: Funding for entrance fees and travel
Spirituality	
1	Personal Renewal: Funding for an annual spiritual retreat
2	Personal Growth: Funding for books / tuition for Scripture exploration
3	Outreach: Funding for a mission trip (2 weeks)
4	Experiential: Funding for a pastored trip to the Holy Lands (Israel)
5	Personal / Internal Healing: Subsidy for spiritual counseling
Philanthropy	
1	Volunteerism: Funding for tutoring wages if performed gratis
2	Service: Funding for travel & expenses for participation in a non-profit project (2 weeks)
3	Opportunity: Provide $500 (inflation adjusted) for special gifts to a person "in-need"
4	Charitable: Funding towards a family foundation, if funding available.
5	Catastrophic Relief: Special natural disaster worldwide relief
Financial	
1	Special Needs: Physical, emotional or mental subsidy.
2	Home Ownership: Funding of a down payment for a first time purchase
3	Entrepreneurship: Funding a venture Capital Fund - 50% maximum participation
4	Family Bank: Loans for home mortgages, asset based financing.
5	Career Selection: Funding for Job Searching Activities/ Programs or Internship Subsidy
Education	
1	Lifelong Learning: Preschool, elementary, Jr/Sr High, college, post grad participation - Max 50%
2	Travel Experience: High School enrichment program; College abroad program, Post college - 1 month "travel pass"
3	Summer Programs: Arts, music, sports, etc.
4	Financial Literacy: Funding for programs to educate/improve money management
5	Knowledge Distribution: Subsidy for self-publishing expenses for authoring books

[62]

B: ATC Administration Agreement

Trust Administration Agreement

4418 S. Technology Dr.
Sioux Falls, SD 57106
605-274-3336

1

For Information Contact Argonne Trust Company at

Client Agreement for Trust Administration

The Client named in this Trust Agreement (the "Agreement") and made part of, (hereinafter, the "Client"), does hereby appoint Argonne Trust Company to act as administrative trustee (the "Trustee") of certain cash, securities and property initially placed in the Client's Trust(s) (the "Trust") with such other cash, securities and property that the Client may deliver to the Trustee or that the Trustee may collect on behalf of the Trust. All such cash, securities and property held from time to time in the Trust are referred to as "Trust Assets".

The Client specifically acknowledges and agrees that with respect to the Client's Investment Advisory Firm / Financial Institution (the "Firm") named in the Application:

a.   The Client and not the Trustee is responsible for investigating and selecting the Firm;

b.   The Firm is not affiliated with or controlled or employed by the Trustee, and the Trustee has not approved, recommended or endorsed the Firm;

c.   The Trustee is not responsible for supervising or monitoring trading by the Firm in the Client's Trust;

d.   The Trustee may provide to the Client's Firm information about investments or investment strategies, but the Client acknowledges that the Trustee does not give tax or legal advice, or advises the Firm on the nature, potential value or suitability for the Client of any particular investments or investment strategies;

e.   The Client has authorized the Firm (or Firms directed by Investment Committee) to be the Client's agent and attorney-in-fact, and in such capacity to provide instructions to Trustee for transactions in the Client's Trust, and to take all other actions necessary or incidental to execution of such instructions. The Firm's authority will include, without limitation, authority to provide instructions to the Trustee for transactions for the Client's benefit, in securities and financial instruments for the Client's Trust, such as stocks, bonds, notes, money market and mutual funds, and other marketable securities and instruments, and authority to provide instructions to the Trustee on any requirements or reallocations of any portfolios selected by the Client, provided, however, in no event shall the Firm be authorized to direct Trustee as Client's attorney-in-fact, to withdraw money, securities or any other assets from Client's Trust without the express written consent of Client's Distribution Committee delivered to Trustee;

f.   The Client agrees that the Trustee will not be liable for any loss, liability, cost or expense for acting upon instructions of the Firm, believed by the Trustee to be genuine in accordance with this Agreement and the Application;

g.   Joint Client understands that each Joint Client authority to transact business individually on behalf of the Trust, as fully and completely as if such Joint Client was the sole owner of the Trust. Subject to Trustee policies, Trustee may accept orders and instructions, written or oral, with respect to the Trust from each Joint Client, without notice to any other Joint Client, or the receipt, transfer, and withdrawal of funds by check, wire transfer, or otherwise and for the purchase, sale, exchange, transfer, or other disposition of Trust Assets. All Joint Client further agree that all Trust Assets that Trustee may be holding for any of them, either in the Trust or otherwise, shall be subject to a lien for the discharge of the obligations of the Trust to the Trustee, such lien to be in addition to any rights and remedies Trustee may otherwise have.

In the event of the death of a Joint Client, divorce of a married Joint Client, assignment of a Joint Client interest, or other event that causes a change of ownership of the trust, all Joint Clients, or the surviving Joint Client(s), as the case may be, shall immediately give Trustee written notice thereof, and Trustee may, in such event, take such action, including requiring such documents or imposing such restrictions on the Trust, as Trustee may deem necessary or appropriate in the circumstances.

The estate of a deceased Joint Client and a departing Joint Client by assignment or divorce shall remain liable, jointly and severally, with the remaining or surviving Joint Client(s), for any obligations of the Trust arising before Trustee receives such notice, or incurred in liquidation of the Trust or the adjustment of the interests of the Joint Clients.

In the event of any such change in ownership of the Trust, Trustee is authorized to divide or redistribute the Trust in accordance with the form of legal ownership of the Trust as reflected in the records of the Trustee, or by proper written instructions of the remaining or surviving Joint Client(s), or by obtaining a court order, as Trustee in its sole discretion may reasonably determine as appropriate in the circumstances. Unless agreed otherwise among the Joint Clients in writing provided to the Trustee, Trusts designated in the Application as "Joint Tenants with Rights of Survivorship" shall vest the interest of a deceased Joint Client in the surviving Joint Client(s), and Trusts designated in the Application as "Tenants in Common" shall

ARGONNE
TRUST COMPANY

Trust Administration Agreement

4418 S. Technology Dr.
Sioux Falls, SD 57106
605-274-3336

2

entitle the estate of a deceased Joint Client to that share of the Trust attributable to the deceased. All Joint Clients agree to indemnify Trustee against any liability, loss, or expense (including attorney's fees) incurred from acting in accordance with Client Agreement and this Amendment in the event of a change in ownership of the Trust.

All statements or other communications sent to or given to one Joint Client by Trustee shall be considered notice to all Joint Clients. In the event Trustee receives inconsistent instructions from two or more Joint Clients, reasonably believes instructions received from one Joint Client are not mutually agreeable to all Joint Clients, or receives a court order with respect to the Trust, Trustee may, but is not obligated to, restrict activity in the Trust, require that all instructions be in writing signed by all Joint Clients and/or file an interpleader action in an appropriate court at the expense of the Joint Clients.

The Client specifically authorizes the Trustee to take all of the following actions with respect to the Trust and Trust Assets:

a. Provide safekeeping for Trust Assets;

b. Buy, sell, redeem, exchange, receive or deliver Trust Assets as directed by the Client's Firm, and pending specific directions from the Firm, invest any cash in such short-term investments as the Trustee deems appropriate including, without limitation, money market funds and repurchase agreements from which the Trustee or its affiliates may receive fees, provided, however, in no event shall the Firm be authorized to direct Trustee, as attorney-in-fact to withdraw money, securities, or any other assets from Client's Trust without the express written consent of Client delivered to Trustee;

c. Disburse cash from the Trust in accordance with instructions properly executed by the Client;

d. Collect income from Trust Assets and deduct and pay all charges and expenses relating to the Trust, including without limitation, the fees of the Firm (charged quarterly is arrears) and the Trustee, brokerage commissions, and any other fees and charges applicable to the Trust;

e. Collect the proceeds of Trust Assets maturing or called for redemption or otherwise payable;

f. Hold registered securities in nominee registration or in street name, as defined on the certificate;

g. Forward voluntary corporate actions, including proxies, to either the Firm to act upon at their discretion, or as otherwise directed by the Client on the Application;

h. Maintain appropriate records of Trust Assets, including all purchases, redemptions, sales and exchanges and furnish monthly statements of transactions to the Client and the Firm;

   1. With respect to all withdrawals from the Trust, Trustee is authorized to rely on instructions, as communicated to Trustee in accordance with Trustee's security verification procedures, without further inquiry or verification of the Client's Distribution Committee identity by Trustee;

   2. All Trust Assets held by Trustee shall be subject to a lien for the discharge of all Client's indebtedness and obligations to Trustee, including any fees and charges owed to Trustee by Client, and are to be held by Trustee as security for the payment of any such indebtedness or obligations in the Trust. Trustee shall have the right to redeem Trust Assets held by Trustee in the Trust to satisfy Client's obligations or indebtedness without further notice or demand. In enforcing its lien, Trustee shall have the discretion to determine which assets in the Trust are to be redeemed and agrees that Trustee shall be held completely harmless from and in any claim, dispute, arbitration or judicial proceeding by reason of its exercise of such discretion.

The Client acknowledges and agrees that Argonne Trust Company, as Trustee, shall continue in full force and effect. Argonne Trust Company represents and warrants that it shall act in compliance with all applicable federal and state laws.

As compensation for its custodial and administrative services, the Trustee shall receive compensation in accordance with its standard schedule of charges, as amended from time to time. The current fee schedule of charges is attached to this Agreement. Changes in such schedule may be effected by the Trustee upon written notice to the Trust.

TRUST COMPANY

Trust Administration Agreement

4418 S. Technology Dr.
Sioux Falls, SD 57106
605-274-3336

3

The Client acknowledges that Trustee prohibits investments by or on behalf of the following persons (each, a "Prohibited Client"): (1) a person whose name appears on the List of Specially Designated Nationals and Blocked Persons maintained by the U.S. Office of Foreign Assets Control ("OFAC"); (2) a foreign shell bank, as defined by the USA Patriot Act; or (3) a person or entity resident in or whose funds are transferred from or through a Trust in a Non-Cooperative Country or Territory, as defined by the Financial Action Task Force.

The Client represents and agrees (1) that all evidence of identity provided is genuine and all related information furnished is accurate; (2) to provide any information deemed necessary by Trustee in its sole discretion to comply with its anti-money laundering program and related responsibilities from time to time; (3) that the Client represents and covenants that neither it, nor any person controlling, controlled by, or under common control with, Trust, or any person having a beneficial interest in Trust, is a Prohibited Client, and that it is not currently or will not open an Trust with Trustee on behalf of or for the benefit of any Prohibited Client agrees to promptly notify Trustee of any change in information affecting this representation and covenant.

The Client acknowledges that investments by the Client may be refused and/or a request for redemption may be delayed or declined if Trustee reasonably believes it does not have satisfactory evidence of Client's identity.

The Client acknowledges that, if, following its trust opening, Trustee reasonably believes that Client is a "Prohibited Client," has otherwise breached its representations and covenants hereunder, or has engaged in a transaction that the Trustee reasonably believes to be suspicious, Trustee may freeze the Client's Trust, prohibit additional investments, decline any redemption requests and/or segregate the assets constituting the investment, redeem or sell the assets, or take any other action reasonably believed to be necessary by Trustee in its sole discretion. Client shall have no claim against Trustee, or its affiliates, for any damages as a result of the aforementioned actions.

The Client elects to waive his or her right to receive a written confirmation of each purchase, redemption, sale or exchange of a security and directs the Trustee to provide basic details of each such transaction by the delivery of monthly statements as provided above.

The Client acknowledges that the Trustee has not made an endorsement or recommendation with respect to the nature or quality of the investments made available to the Client and that Trust Assets are not the Trustee's obligation and are not insured by the Federal Deposit Insurance Corporation. Further, the Client understands that neither the value of Trust Assets nor their rates of return are guaranteed.

The Client agrees to hold the Trustee harmless against and indemnify and reimburse the Trustee for any liability, loss, damage or expense (including attorney's fees) incurred any way in connection with the Trust or Trust Assets except where such loss or damage directly results from gross negligence or willful misconduct of the Trustee.

The Trustee shall not be under any obligation to defend any legal action or engage in any legal proceedings with respect to the Trust.

This Agreement shall be governed under the laws of the state of South Dakota and may be modified only in writing, executed by both the Client and the Trustee. Each party may terminate this Agreement at any time by giving at least ten (10) days written notice to the other to that effect. Trustee may transfer or assign its right and obligations under this agreement upon ten (10) days written notice to Client. Notwithstanding the foregoing, Trustee may terminate this agreement at any time, without prior written notice to Client, if Trustee believes that Client is a "Prohibited Client," or Client has engaged in a transaction that the Trustee reasonably believes to be suspicious.

Signatures

This application **must** be signed by the Client and acknowledged by the Firm named on this Trust Application. By signing this Trust Application, the Client authorizes the Trustee to act on instructions received from the Firm in accordance with the **Client Agreement**, and hereby confirms that the Firm is authorized to give such instructions. This Trust Agreement shall remain in effect until revoked, modified or amended by the Client upon 10 days prior written notice to the Trustee.

ARGONNE
TRUST COMPANY

Trust Administration Agreement

4418 S. Technology Dr.
Sioux Falls, SD 57106
605-274-3336

4

By signing this Trust Agreement and Application the Client hereby certifies under penalties of perjury that the information contained within this agreement is complete and correct, and that:

A.   The Taxpayer ID Number or Social Security Number shown is correct, or the taxpayer is waiting for a number.

B.   I am a U.S. person (including a U.S. resident alien).

C.   _____ Check here if the Client is subject to backup withholding under the provisions of Section 3406(a)(1) of the Internal Revenue Code.

The Internal Revenue Service does not require your consent to any provision of this document other than the certifications required to avoid backup withholding

Client's Name _____

 Client's Signature _____   Date _____

Name of Joint Owner (if applicable) _____

 Signature of Joint Owner (if applicable) _____   Date _____

Investment Advisory Firm:

Name (state whether Advisor or Consultant) _____

Signature _____   Date _____

Argonne Trust Company:

Authorized Signature _____   Date _____

Note: All signatures are required to open a Trust. If the appropriate signatures are not received, the Trust will not be opened and any initial funding will not be invested until all signatures are received.

Please be sure that:
· All sections of the Application have been completed
· All appropriate parties have completed and have signed the application, including joint owner(s), guardian/conservator, trustee(s) of minor, co-trustee(s), co-executor(s), and Organization Representative(s). (If applicable)
· All required documents have been included (if applicable)
· All pages of Client Application and Agreement are enclosed
      Failure to provide all information and/or documentation may result in processing delays or return of paperwork.

ARGONNE
TRUST COMPANY

Trust Administration Agreement

4418 S. Technology Dr.
Sioux Falls, SD 57106
605-274-3336

5

Independent Trustee Certification

All Independent Trustees must sign this section. Please indicate in Section B the number of signatures required to act on the Argonne Trust Company trust. If a number is not indicated, the signature of one Trustee will be required on transaction requests. **If the Trustee is an organization, a certified Argonne Trust Company Corporate/Organization Resolution Form is also required.**

Please submit the following:

• Page of Trust document that appoints the Independent Trustee and all signatory and notary pages. In the case of a Trust established under a will, Argonne Trust Company would need this information from the will document.

A. Trust Information

Name of Trust _____

B. Number of signatures required to transact

Indicate the number of Trustee signatures required to act on the Trust. If a number is not indicated, the signature of one Trustee will be required on transaction requests.

Number of Trustee signatures required: _____

C. Indemnification

All trustees must sign; each Independent Trustee's printed name and signature must match.

The undersigned are duly appointed Independent Trustees of _____
_____ Name of Trust.

_____ Trust's Taxpayer Identification Number or Social Security Number

The Independent Trustees agree, on behalf of the Trust, to indemnify and hold Argonne Trust Company harmless from acting upon the instructions believed to have originated from the Independent Trustees named below. The undersigned are duly authorized by Trust provisions to act on behalf of this Trust in connection with the Argonne Trust Company Trust owned by this Trust. The Trustees named below are authorized: 1) to invest the assets of the Trust; 2) to give instructions for the purchase, sale, exchange or transfer of securities; and 3) to execute any necessary forms in connection with those securities.

The undersigned Independent Trustees certify that there are no additional Trustees of this Trust.

This certification is to remain in full force and effect until revoked in writing by the Independent Trustees listed below and delivered to Argonne Trust Company. The revocation will not affect any action taken before Argonne Trust Company has had a reasonable amount of time to act upon the revocation. Attach an additional sheet if there are more than four Independent Trustees.

Name of Independent Trustee_____ Signature _____

Name of Independent Trustee_____ Signature _____

Name of Independent Trustee_____ Signature _____

Name of Independent Trustee_____ Signature _____

[67]

Trust Administration Agreement

4418 S. Technology Dr.
Sioux Falls, SD 57106
605-274-3336

6

Please describe on this final page any special requirements, relating to the sale or disposition of real estate, closely held business interests, or the purchase of such assets by the Trustee. Indicate who is expected to perform any special tasks involved in establishing, funding or managing the Trust.

In addition, in cases of Elder Care issues, please describe the circumstances of the Grantor(s) and the goals that are to be achieved by the creation and funding of the Trust.

If there are special needs heirs, or circumstances surrounding family circumstances, such as unique marital relationships, non-citizen spouses, goals with regard to asset protection, or any other concerns that need special attention and that Argonne Trust needs to know, please also explain those issues here.

4418 S. Technology Dr.
Sioux Falls, SD 57106
605-274-3336

Email
info@ArgonneTrust.com

www.ArgonneTrust.com

4418 S. Technology Dr.
Sioux Falls, SD 57106
605-274-3336

Exhibit A:

C: Job Descriptions for a SD Purposeful Trust:

- **Grantor** – This is the individual who can initially make contributions into the trust. Only upon the death of the grantor can other individuals make additional contributions into the trust. The Grantor may not receive any distribution (income or principal) from the trust. Hence, the assets which are placed into the trust should be those which are not necessary to maintain the Grantor's standard of living.

- **Beneficiaries** – This trust is unique in that the beneficiaries are a "class" that is made up of the current and future heirs of the Grantor. South Dakota allows for the beneficiary to be a "purpose" and the beneficiaries have no ownership of the trust assets but rather simply stewardship (care and usage) of the trust assets.

- **Trust Protector** - This is the most powerful individual position in the trust. It may not be a family member or a business associate, but a trusted advisor. (It may be a business entity, such as the trusted advisor's LLC.) The main duties are to appoint or replace the Trustee Appointer, the Investment Committee members and the Distribution Committee members. This individual is to provide an oversight of the positions ensuring that they are fulfilling their duties in an appropriate manner.

- **Trust Company** – This is a South Dakota (bank department chartered) trust company that is responsible for the day to day compliance and administration of the trust. The trust company is compensated based on the amount and composition of the investments in the trust (i.e. closely held business, income producing real estate, residential real estate, etc.).

- **Investment Committee** – This can be made up of either a Registered Investment Advisory firm or family members (or combination of both). They are responsible for the investing (based on Prudent Investor Rules) of the marketable securities within the trust. The investment advisory firm is entitled to an investment management fee.

- **Distribution Committee**– This group cannot be made up of beneficiaries. It can be a trusted advisor, but most likely will be the trust company. The function is to make appropriate payments from and for the trust, as per the trust provisions.

- **Purposeful Trust Attorney** – This is a group in the legal profession that specialize in the creation of trusts to perpetuate "values," not simply valuables.

- **Family Advisor** – This is a recent SD development (7/1/2016) that provides for the position of "family advisor" to consult with or advise the other fiduciaries (including trustees, distribution advisors, or investment advisors) in a non-fiduciary capacity. The family advisor may only exercise four powers set forth in Section 18 if provided in the governing instrument, which are;
- removal and appointment of fiduciaries or advisors, appointment of successors,
- advise the trustee on matters concerning a beneficiary,
- consult with a fiduciary, and
- provide direction regarding notice to qualified beneficiaries, in the family advisor's sole discretion.

D: IRS Form 8938

Form **8938**	Statement of Specified Foreign Financial Assets	OMB No. 1545-2195
(Rev. December 2014) Department of the Treasury Internal Revenue Service	▶ Information about Form 8938 and its separate instructions is at www.irs.gov/form8938. ▶ Attach to your tax return. For calendar year 20 ____ or tax year beginning ____ , 20 ____ and ending ____ , 20 ____	Attachment Sequence No. 175

If you have attached continuation statements, check here ☐   Number of continuation statements _____

Name(s) shown on return _____   TIN _____

Part I   Foreign Deposit and Custodial Accounts Summary

1	Number of Deposit Accounts (reported on Form 8938)	▶	
2	Maximum Value of All Deposit Accounts	$	
3	Number of Custodial Accounts (reported on Form 8938)	▶	
4	Maximum Value of All Custodial Accounts	$	
5	Were any foreign deposit or custodial accounts closed during the tax year?	☐ Yes	☐ No

Part II   Other Foreign Assets Summary

1	Number of Foreign Assets (reported on Form 8938)	▶	
2	Maximum Value of All Assets	$	
3	Were any foreign assets acquired or sold during the tax year?	☐ Yes	☐ No

Part III   Summary of Tax Items Attributable to Specified Foreign Financial Assets (see instructions)

(a) Asset Category	(b) Tax item		(c) Amount reported on form or schedule	Where reported	
				(d) Form and line	(e) Schedule and line
1 Foreign Deposit and Custodial Accounts	1a	Interest	$		
	1b	Dividends	$		
	1c	Royalties	$		
	1d	Other income	$		
	1e	Gains (losses)	$		
	1f	Deductions	$		
	1g	Credits	$		
2 Other Foreign Assets	2a	Interest	$		
	2b	Dividends	$		
	2c	Royalties	$		
	2d	Other income	$		
	2e	Gains (losses)	$		
	2f	Deductions	$		
	2g	Credits	$		

Part IV   Excepted Specified Foreign Financial Assets (see instructions)

If you reported specified foreign financial assets on one or more of the following forms, enter the number of such forms filed. You do not need to include these assets on Form 8938 for the tax year.

| 1. Number of Forms 3520 ____ | 2. Number of Forms 3520-A ____ | 3. Number of Forms 5471 ____ |
| 4. Number of Forms 8621 ____ | 5. Number of Forms 8865 ____ | 6. Number of Forms 8891 ____ |

Part V   Detailed Information for Each Foreign Deposit and Custodial Account Included in the Part I Summary (see instructions)

If you have more than one account to report, attach a continuation statement for each additional account (see instructions).

1	Type of account	☐ Deposit ☐ Custodial	2	Account number or other designation

3	Check all that apply	a ☐ Account opened during tax year	b ☐ Account closed during tax year
		c ☐ Account jointly owned with spouse	d ☐ No tax item reported in Part III with respect to this asset
4	Maximum value of account during tax year		$
5	Did you use a foreign currency exchange rate to convert the value of the account into U.S. dollars?	☐ Yes ☐ No
6	If you answered "Yes" to line 5, complete all that apply.		

(a) Foreign currency in which account is maintained	(b) Foreign currency exchange rate used to convert to U.S. dollars	(c) Source of exchange rate used if not from U.S. Treasury Financial Management Service

For Paperwork Reduction Act Notice, see the separate instructions.   Cat. No. 37753A   Form **8938** (Rev. 12-2014)

Part V   Detailed Information for Each Foreign Deposit and Custodial Account Included in the Part I Summary (see instructions) (continued)

7a   Name of financial institution in which account is maintained   **b** Reserved

8   Mailing address of financial institution in which account is maintained. Number, street, and room or suite no.

9   City or town, state or province, and country (including postal code)

Part VI   Detailed Information for Each "Other Foreign Asset" Included in the Part II Summary (see instructions)

Note. If you reported specified foreign financial assets on Forms 3520, 3520-A, 5471, 8621, 8865, or 8891, you do not have to include the assets on Form 8938. You must complete Part IV. See instructions.

If you have more than one asset to report, attach a continuation statement for each additional asset (see instructions).

1   Description of asset   2   Identifying number or other designation

3   Complete all that apply. See instructions for reporting of multiple acquisition or disposition dates.
a   Date asset acquired during tax year, if applicable . . . .
b   Date asset disposed of during tax year, if applicable . . . .
c   ☐ Check if asset jointly owned with spouse   d   ☐ Check if no tax item reported in Part III with respect to this asset

4   Maximum value of asset during tax year (check box that applies)
a   ☐ $0 - $50,000   b   ☐ $50,001 - $100,000   c   ☐ $100,001 - $150,000   d   ☐ $150,001 - $200,000
e   If more than $200,000, list value $

5   Did you use a foreign currency exchange rate to convert the value of the asset into U.S. dollars? . . .   ☐ Yes   ☐ No

6   If you answered "Yes" to line 5, complete all that apply.
(a) Foreign currency in which asset is denominated   **(b)** Foreign currency exchange rate used to convert to U.S. dollars   **(c)** Source of exchange rate used if not from U.S. Treasury Financial Management Service

7   If asset reported on line 1 is stock of a foreign entity or an interest in a foreign entity, enter the following information for the asset.
a   Name of foreign entity   **b** Reserved
c   Type of foreign entity   (1) ☐ Partnership   (2) ☐ Corporation   (3) ☐ Trust   (4) ☐ Estate
d   Mailing address of foreign entity. Number, street, and room or suite no.

e   City or town, state or province, and country (including postal code)

8   If asset reported on line 1 is not stock of a foreign entity or an interest in a foreign entity, enter the following information for the asset.
Note. If this asset has more than one issuer or counterparty, attach a continuation statement with the same information for each additional issuer or counterparty (see instructions).

a   Name of issuer or counterparty
   Check if information is for   ☐ Issuer   ☐ Counterparty

b   Type of issuer or counterparty
   (1) ☐ Individual   (2) ☐ Partnership   (3) ☐ Corporation   (4) ☐ Trust   (5) ☐ Estate

c   Check if issuer or counterparty is a   ☐ U.S. person   ☐ Foreign person
d   Mailing address of issuer or counterparty. Number, street, and room or suite no.

e   City or town, state or province, and country (including postal code)

                                          Form **8938** (Rev. 12-2014)

E: Articles

The World's Favorite New Tax Haven Is the US

Bloomberg   By Jesse Drucker,   Jan. 27, 2016

Last September, at a law firm overlooking San Francisco Bay, Andrew Penney, a managing director at Rothschild & Co., gave a talk on how the world's wealthy elite can avoid paying taxes.

His message was clear: You can help your clients move their fortunes to the United States, free of taxes and hidden from their governments.

Some are calling it the new Switzerland.

After years of lambasting other countries for helping rich Americans hide their money offshore, the U.S. is emerging as a leading tax and secrecy haven for rich foreigners. By resisting new global disclosure standards, the U.S. is creating a hot new market, becoming the go-to place to stash foreign wealth. Everyone from London lawyers to Swiss trust companies is getting in on the act, helping the world's rich move accounts from places like the Bahamas and the British Virgin Islands to Nevada, Wyoming, and South Dakota.

"How ironic—no, how perverse—that the USA, which has been so sanctimonious in its condemnation of Swiss banks, has become the banking secrecy jurisdiction du jour," wrote Peter A. Cotorceanu, a lawyer at Anaford AG, a Zurich law firm, in a recent legal journal. "That 'giant sucking sound' you hear? It is the sound of money rushing to the USA."

Rothschild, the centuries-old European financial institution, has opened a trust company in Reno, Nev., a few blocks from the Harrah's and Eldorado casinos. It is now moving the fortunes of wealthy foreign clients out of offshore havens such as Bermuda, subject to the new international disclosure requirements, and into Rothschild-run trusts in Nevada, which are exempt.

The U.S. "is effectively the biggest tax haven in the world" —*Andrew Penney, Rothschild & Co.*

The firm says its Reno operation caters to international families attracted to the stability of the U.S. and that customers must prove they comply with their home countries' tax laws. Its trusts, moreover, have "not been set up with a view to exploiting that the U.S. has not signed up" for international reporting standards, said Rothschild spokeswoman Emma Rees.

Others are also jumping in: Geneva-based Cisa Trust Co. SA, which advises wealthy Latin Americans, is applying to open in Pierre, S.D., to "serve the needs of our foreign clients," said John J. Ryan Jr., Cisa's president.

Trident Trust Co., one of the world's biggest providers of offshore trusts, moved dozens of accounts out of Switzerland, Grand Cayman, and other locales and into Sioux Falls, S.D., in December, ahead of a Jan. 1 disclosure deadline.

"Cayman was slammed in December, closing things that people were withdrawing," said Alice Rokahr, the president of Trident in South Dakota, one of several states promoting low taxes and confidentiality in their trust laws. "I was surprised at how many were coming across that were formerly Swiss bank accounts, but they want out of Switzerland."

Rokahr and other advisers said there is a legitimate need for secrecy. Confidential accounts that hide wealth, whether in the U.S., Switzerland, or elsewhere, protect against kidnappings or extortion in their owners' home countries. The rich also often feel safer parking their money in the U.S. rather than some other location perceived as less-sure.

"I do not hear anybody saying, 'I want to avoid taxes,' " Rokahr said. "These are people who are legitimately concerned with their own health and welfare."

No one expects offshore havens to disappear anytime soon. Swiss banks still hold about $1.9 trillion in assets not reported by account holders in their home countries, according to Gabriel Zucman, an economics professor at the University of California at Berkeley. Nor is it clear how many of the almost 100 countries and other jurisdictions that have signed on will actually enforce the new disclosure standards, issued by the Organisation for Economic Co-operation and Development, a government-funded international policy group.

There's nothing illegal about banks luring foreigners to put money in the U.S. with promises of confidentiality as long as they are not intentionally helping to evade taxes abroad. Still, the U.S. is one of the few places left where advisers are actively promoting accounts that will remain secret from overseas authorities.

Rothschild's Reno office is at the forefront of that effort. "The Biggest Little City in the World" is not an obvious choice for a global center of capital flight. If you were going to shoot a film set in Las Vegas circa 1971, you would film it in Reno. Its casino hotels tower above the bail bondsmen across the street, available 24/7, as well as pawnshops stocked with an array of firearms. The pink neon lights at casinos like Harrah's and the Eldorado still burn bright. But these days, their floors are often empty, with travelers preferring to gamble in Las Vegas, an hour's flight away.

The offices of Rothschild Trust North America LLC aren't easy to find. They're on the 12th floor of Porsche's former North American headquarters building, a few blocks from the casinos. (The U.S. attorney's office is on the sixth floor.) Yet the lobby directory does not list Rothschild. Instead, visitors must go to the 10th floor, the offices of McDonald Carano Wilson LLP, a politically connected law firm. Several former high-ranking Nevada state officials work there, as well as the owner of some of Reno's biggest casinos and numerous registered lobbyists. One of the firm's tax lobbyists is Robert Armstrong, viewed as the state's top trusts and estates attorney, and a manager of Rothschild Trust North America.

The trust company was set up in 2013 to cater to <u>international families, particularly those with a mix of assets and relatives in the U.S.</u> and abroad, according to Rothschild. It caters to customers attracted to the "stable, regulated environment" of the U.S., said Rees, the Rothschild spokeswoman.

"We do not offer legal structures to clients unless we are absolutely certain that their tax affairs are in order; both clients themselves and independent tax lawyers must actively confirm to us that this is the case," Rees said.

The managing director of the Nevada trust company is Scott Cripps, an amiable California tax attorney who used to run the trust services for Bank of the West, now part of French financial-services giant BNP Paribas SA. Cripps explained that moving money out of traditional offshore secrecy jurisdictions and into Nevada is a brisk new line of business for Rothschild.

"There's a lot of people that are going to do it," said Cripps. "This added layer of privacy is kicking them over the hurdle" to move their assets into the U.S. For wealthy overseas clients, "privacy is huge, especially in countries where there is corruption."

One wealthy Turkish family is using Rothschild's trust company to move assets from the Bahamas into the U.S., he said. Another Rothschild client, a family from Asia, is moving assets from Bermuda into Nevada. He said customers are often international families with offspring in the U.S.

For decades, Switzerland has been the global capital of secret bank accounts. That may be changing. In 2007, UBS Group AG banker Bradley Birkenfeld blew the whistle on his firm helping U.S. clients evade taxes with undeclared accounts offshore. Swiss banks eventually paid a price. More than 80 Swiss banks, including UBS and Credit Suisse Group AG, have agreed to pay about $5 billion to the U.S. in penalties and fines.

"I was surprised at how many were coming across that were formerly Swiss bank accounts, but they want out of Switzerland"

Those firms also include Rothschild Bank AG, which last June entered into a non-prosecution agreement with the U.S. Department of Justice. The bank admitted helping U.S. clients hide income offshore from the Internal Revenue Service and agreed to pay an $11.5 million penalty and shut down nearly 300 accounts belonging to U.S. taxpayers, totaling $794 million in assets.

The U.S. was determined to put an end to such practices. That led to a 2010 law, the Foreign Account Tax Compliance Act, or FATCA, that requires financial firms to disclose foreign accounts held by U.S. citizens and report them to the IRS or face steep penalties.

Inspired by FACTA, the OECD drew up even stiffer standards to help other countries ferret out tax dodgers. Since 2014, 97 jurisdictions have agreed to impose new disclosure requirements for bank accounts, trusts, and some other investments held by international customers. Of the nations the OECD asked to sign on, only a handful have declined: Bahrain, Nauru, Vanuatu—and the United States.

"I have a lot of respect for the Obama administration because without their first moves we would not have gotten these reporting standards," said Sven Giegold, a member of the European Parliament from Germany's Green Party. "On the other hand, now it's time for the U.S. to deliver what Europeans are willing to deliver to the U.S."

The Treasury Department makes no apologies for not agreeing to the OECD standards.

"The U.S. has led the charge in combating international tax evasion using offshore financial accounts," said Treasury spokesman Ryan Daniels. He said the OECD initiative "builds directly" on the FACTA law.

For financial advisers, the current state of play is simply a good business opportunity. In a draft of his San Francisco presentation, Rothschild's Penney wrote that the U.S. "is effectively the biggest tax haven in the world." The U.S., he added in language later excised from his prepared remarks, lacks "the resources to enforce foreign tax laws and has little appetite to do so."

Firms aren't wasting time to make the most of the current environment. Bolton Global Capital, a Boston-area financial advisory firm, recently circulated this hypothetical example in an e-mail: A wealthy Mexican opens a U.S. bank account using a company in the

British Virgin Islands. As a result, only the company's name would be sent to the BVI government, while the identity of the person owning the account would not be shared with Mexican authorities.

The U.S. failure to sign onto the OECD information-sharing standard is "proving to be a strong driver of growth for our business," wrote Bolton's chief executive officer, Ray Grenier, in a marketing e-mail to bankers. His firm is seeing a spike in accounts moved out of European banks—"Switzerland in particular"—and into the U.S. The new OECD standard "was the beginning of the exodus," he said in an interview.

The U.S. Treasury is proposing standards similar to the OECD's for foreign-held accounts in the U.S. But similar proposals in the past have stalled in the face of opposition from the Republican-controlled Congress and the banking industry.

At issue is not just non-U.S. citizens skirting their home countries' taxes. Treasury also is concerned that massive inflows of capital into secret accounts could become a new channel for criminal money laundering. At least $1.6 trillion in illicit funds are laundered through the global financial system each year, according to a United Nations estimate.

Offering secrecy to clients is not against the law, but U.S. firms are not permitted to knowingly help overseas customers evade foreign taxes, said Scott Michel, a criminal tax defense attorney at Washington, D.C.-based Caplin & Drysdale who has represented Swiss banks and foreign account holders.

"To the extent non-U.S. persons are encouraged to come to the U.S. for what may be our own 'tax haven' characteristics, the U.S.

government would likely take a dim view of any marketing suggesting that evading home country tax is a legal objective," he said.

Rothschild says it takes "significant care" to ensure account holders' assets are fully declared. The bank "adheres to the legal, regulatory, and tax rules wherever we operate," said Rees, the Rothschild spokeswoman.

Penney, who oversees the Reno business, is a longtime Rothschild lawyer who worked his way up from the firm's trust operations in the tiny British isle of Guernsey. Penney, 56, is now a managing director based in London for Rothschild Wealth Management & Trust, which handles about $23 billion for 7,000 clients from offices including Milan, Zurich, and Hong Kong. A few years ago he was voted "Trustee of the Year" by an elite group of U.K. wealth advisers.

In his September San Francisco talk, called "Using U.S. Trusts in International Planning: 10 Amazing Feats to Impress Clients and Colleagues," Penney laid out legal ways to avoid both U.S. taxes and disclosures to clients' home countries.

In a section originally titled "U.S. Trusts to Preserve Privacy," he included the hypothetical example of an Internet investor named "Wang, a Hong Kong resident," originally from the People's Republic of China, concerned that information about his wealth could be shared with Chinese authorities.

Putting his assets into a Nevada (or South Dakota) LLC, in turn owned by a Nevada (or South Dakota) trust, would generate no U.S. tax returns, Penney wrote. Any forms the IRS would receive would result in "no meaningful information to exchange under" agreements between Hong Kong and the U.S., according to Penney's PowerPoint presentation reviewed by Bloomberg.

Penney offered a disclaimer: At least one government, the U.K., intends to make it a criminal offense for any U.K. firm to facilitate tax evasion.

Rothschild said the PowerPoint was subsequently revised before Penney delivered his presentation. The firm provided what it said was the final version of the talk, which this time excluded several potentially controversial passages. Among them: the U.S. being the "biggest tax haven in the world," the U.S.'s low appetite for enforcing other countries' tax laws, and two references to "privacy" offered by the U.S.

"The presentation was drafted in response to a request by the organizers to be controversial and create a lively debate among the experienced, professional audience," Rees said. "On reviewing the initial draft, these lines were not deemed to represent either Rothschild's or Mr. Penney's view. They were therefore removed."
—With assistance from David Voreacos and Patrick Gower

F: Resources

Books by Roey Diefendorf

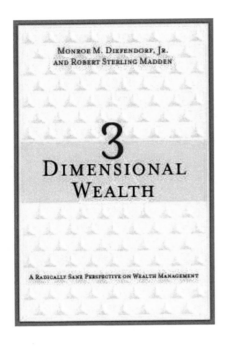

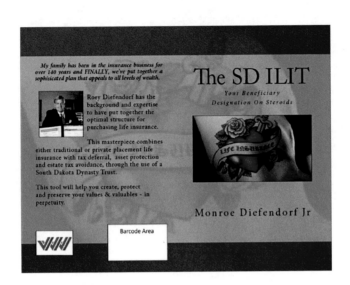

My family has been in the insurance business for over 140 years and FINALLY, we've put together a sophisicated plan that appeals to all levels of wealth.

Roey Diefendorf has the background and expertise to have put together the optimal structure for purchasing life insurance.

This masterpiece combines either traditional or private placement life insurance with tax deferral, asset protection and estate tax avoidance, through the use of a South Dakota Dynasty Trust.

This tool will help you create, protect and preserve your values & valuables - in perpetuity.

Barcode Area

The SD ILIT

Your Beneficiary Designation On Steroids

Monroe Diefendorf Jr

ROEY DIEFENDORF IS THE CEO OF ARGONNE TRUST COMPANY OF SOUTH DAKOTA. BECAUSE OF THE UNIQUE STATUES IN SD, IT IS BEING CALLED "THE NEW SWITZERLAND." IRONIC THAT SOUTH DAKOTA IS BECOMING THE FAVORED TAX HAVEN THROUGHOUT THE GLOBE. LEARN HOW YOU CAN BENEFIT FROM US DOMICILED TRUSTS.

Barcode Area

US TRUSTS FOR FOREIGN NATIONALS

SOUTH DAKOTA
THE ONE & ONLY

MONROE DIEFENDORF, JR

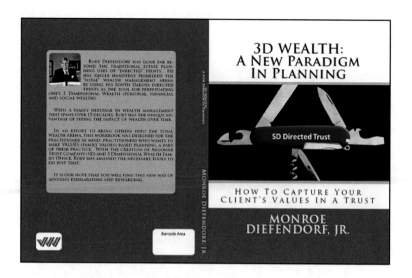

Disclosures

The information in this booklet is intended to serve as a basis for discussion with financial, legal, tax and/or accounting advisors. It is not a substitute for competent advice from these advisors. The actual application of some of these concepts may be the practice of law and is the proper responsibility of an attorney. The application of other concepts may require the guidance of a tax or accounting advisor.

Although great effort has been taken to provide accurate numbers and explanations, the information in this report should not be relied upon for preparing tax returns or making investment decisions. Assumed rates of return are not in any way to be taken as guaranteed projections of actual returns from any recommended investment opportunity. If a numerical analysis is shown, the results are neither guarantees nor projections, and actual results may differ significantly. Any assumptions as to interest rates, rates of return, inflation, or other values are hypothetical and for illustrative purposes only. Rates of return shown are not indicative of any particular investment, and will vary over time. Any reference to past performance is not indicative of future results and should not be taken as a guaranteed projection of actual returns from any recommended investment.

The company or companies listed below are not authorized to practice law or to provide legal, tax, or accounting advice.

This information in this booklet has neither been audited by nor verified by the company, or companies, listed below and is therefore not guaranteed by them as to its accuracy.

ATC Directory

ARGONNE TRUST COMPANY

DIRECTORY

4418 S. Technology Drive, Sioux Falls

1-800-521-0267

Service Requests:	Service@ArgonneTrust.com
Distribution Requests:	Distributions@ArgonneTrust.com
Tax Questions:	Tax@ArgonneTrust.com

Trust Officer:

JoAnn Dickinson, JD, CTFA   JoAnn@ArgonneTrust.com

Trust Marketing Officers:

Monroe Diefendorf, Jr, Pres., CEO	Roey@ArgonneTrust.com
Demetri Doumas, Tres.	Demetri@ArgonneTrust.com
Jeffrey Higgs, Sec.	Jeff@ArgonneTrust.com
Steven Howe	Steve@ArgonneTrust.com
Thomas Palumbo	Tom@ArgonneTrust.com
David Taylor	David@ArgonneTrust.com

Biography

Monroe M. "Roey" Diefendorf, Jr. is a 46 year veteran wealth manager in Locust Valley, NY.

Roey graduated from Deerfield Academy and Bucknell University where he received his degree in psychology. Roey has a Masters in Insurance from Georgia State University. He has completed the CLU,  ChFC, RFC, CFP, CIMA and CAP designations over his career.

Roey has developed his national reputation in the "total" wealth management arena with the introduction of first two books "*3 Dimensional Wealth: A Radically Sane Perspective On Wealth Management*" and "*A Better Way: Using Purposeful Trusts To Preserve Values & Valuables In Perpetuity*". In addition, he has authored, "*South Dakota, USA – 57106: The Preferred Jurisdiction For Your Trust Needs*" and "*3D Wealth: A New Paradigm In Planning – How to capture your client's values in a trust*", "*The SD ILIT: Your Beneficiary Designation of Steroids*", and "*US Trusts for Foreign Nationals: South Dakota – The One & Only.*"

Roey has also co-authored "*Private Placement Life Insurance: A Sophisticated Investment Solution for High Net Worth Investors*" and "*Private Placement Variable Annuity: A Sophisticated Investment Solution for High Net Worth Investors*" with Gerald Nowotny, JD, LLM.

Roey is the Chief Executive Officer of 3 Dimensional Wealth Advisory, LLC *(formerly Diefendorf Capital Planning Associates)*. He founded both Argonne Trust Company, Inc. (SD) and the Monroe Insurance Dedicated Funds (DE) bringing values based solutions to the domestic PPLI marketplace, as well as, the traditional insurance arena.

For More Information

3 Dimensional Wealth Advisory, LLC

152 Forest Avenue, Locust Valley, NY 11560

1-877-3D-Wealth

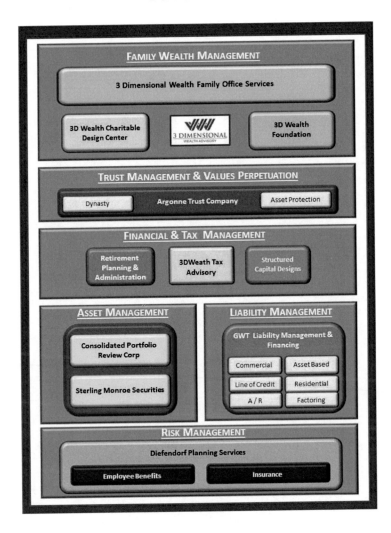